THE THIRD GENERATION

*Young Conservative Leaders
Look to the Future*

THE THIRD GENERATION

Edited by
Benjamin Hart

Regnery Books, Washington, D.C.

Copyright © 1987 by The Heritage Foundation

All rights reserved. No part of this publication may be reproduced or transmitted in any form or by any means, electronic or mechanical, including photocopy, recording, or any information storage and retrieval system now known or to be invented, without permission in writing from the publisher, except by a reviewer who wishes to quote brief passages in connection with a review written for inclusion in a magazine, newspaper, or broadcast.

Library of Congress Cataloging-in-Publication Data

The Third generation.

Bibliography: p. 255-270
1. Conservatism—United States. I. Hart, Benjamin.
JA84.U5T455   1987   320.5'2'0973   87-4540

Published in the United States by
Regnery Gateway
1130 17th Street, NW
Washington DC 20036

Distributed to the trade by
Kampmann & Company, Inc.
9 E. 40th Street
New York NY 10016

10 9 8 7 6 5 4 3 2 1

*To
Clare Boothe Luce*

ACKNOWLEDGMENTS

I thank Heritage's Ed Feulner, Phil Truluck, and Burt Pines, without whose vision, encouragement, and support there would be no Third Generation. They are the role models to whom young conservative activists, policy-makers, and intellectuals in Washington look for leadership.

CONTENTS

Introduction: What Is the Third Generation?	11
1. THE REAGAN REVOLUTION: FACT OR FANTASY?	29
2. WHY CONSERVATIVE IDEAS SHOULD ATTRACT BLACK AMERICANS.	47
3. GOING ON THE MORAL OFFENSIVE.	67
4. FAITH AND POLITICS.	79
5. CHURCH, SCHOOL, FAMILY, AND THE STATE	92
6. ROLLING BACK THE EVIL EMPIRE	107
7. DISMANTLING THE WELFARE STATE	123
8. THE WAR IN THE TRENCHES	138
9. A CONSERVATIVE NEW DEAL	149
10. THE AMERICAN CAMPUS IN EXILE	168
11. WHITHER LIBERALISM?	175
12. THE RADICAL CASE FOR FREEDOM	187
13. SOME WORDS OF CAUTION	208
14. A TRIBUTE TO BARRY GOLDWATER	217
15. *The Participants*	223
16. *A Conservative Heritage*	255

"The greatest days of the conservative movement lie ahead . . . One of the best omens for conservatives is that growing numbers of young men and women in their twenties and thirties share basic beliefs in the need to defend freedom, preserve the sanctity of human life, and limit the size and scope of government. This so-called 'Third Generation' of conservatives is extraordinarily well-equipped—in terms of commitment, education, and professional experience—to promote the issues and values that are the bedrock of our movement."

Ronald Reagan
PRESIDENT OF THE UNITED STATES

INTRODUCTION: WHAT IS THE THIRD GENERATION?

It was November of 1983. The Heritage Foundation had recently moved into a large, eight-story building on Capitol Hill, occupying four of its floors. The remaining office space was in the process of being leased to various political groups, lobbying organizations, and think tanks, the majority of which were conservative. What we at Heritage discovered, after a few months in the new building, was that a majority of those renting offices and attending Heritage-sponsored conferences and roundtable discussions seemed to be in their twenties and early thirties.

"Who are they?" asked Heritage Vice President Burt Pines. "There seem to be hundreds of young people in town—writers, self-proclaimed experts on policy, heads of organizations, congressional chiefs of staff, key people in the Administration. They're in the building, carrying briefcases, hosting freedom fighters, and holding strategy meetings. I have almost no idea who they are. We must get to know them."

"I've been in this policy business since the Draft Goldwater Movement," Heritage President Ed Feulner remarked. "Before Reagan won in 1980, all the conservatives in town could meet for lunch. Today, there seem to be literally thousands, many of whom can't remember Vietnam, much less the Goldwater campaign."

We decided it would be useful to identify the young leaders of this army of conservative activists, political strategists, administrators, and intellectuals who invaded Washington in the wake of Ronald Reagan's 1980 landslide victory. To remain vibrant and fresh, the conservative movement would have to encourage the emergence of new leaders. At that time, the fall of 1983, there was no systematic effort to identify young conservative talent in Washington. There was no regularly scheduled forum or meeting place where people could convene to hear the views of these young activists and thinkers.

It was to provide such a forum that Heritage initiated the Third Generation Project. The first meeting was held on a snowy evening in January 1984. Seventeen young conservatives, who were working in various capacities in Washington's political and policy-making establishments, arrived to listen to Dinesh D'Souza talk about why conservatives had failed so dismally in getting a fair hearing for their views in the prestige media. Then age 23, D'Souza already had established himself as one of the most promising journalists of his generation. His talk and the meeting in general apparently were a success.

Two weeks later, at the second gathering, 35 people arrived to hear Frank Cannon, who was working for Duncan Hunter, a Republican congressman from California, speak on "How the Third Generation Can Win on Capitol Hill." Only 25 at the time, Cannon was the youngest chief of staff in Congress. The third meeting, two Wednesdays later, had to be moved from the Heritage building's seventh floor Shelby Cullom Davis Policy Center into the Lehrman Auditorium, as 65 young conservatives came to listen to Amy Moritz, then the 25-year-old executive director of the National Center for Public Policy Research, talk on "How to Moblize the Third Generation."

From then on, the fortnightly Third Generation gatherings began drawing crowds in excess of 100 young men and women, mainly from congressional offices, the White House and Administration, think tanks, campaign organizations, and an assortment of publications dealing with politics and policy.

The forums were attractive because they produced lively discussions that often grew into heated debates, probing the corners of conservative thinking and sometimes testing the patience of Third Generation members. The Old Right did not always agree with the neoconservatives, and sometimes the New Right came into conflict with the libertarians, who in turn had some fundamental problems with the classical liberals.

A typical such exchange occurred in the spring of 1984. Walter Olson, then 27, an editor of the American Enterprise Institute's *Regulation* magazine, an associate editor of *National Review,* and a libertarian, was speaking on "The Role of Libertarians in the Third Generation." He was in the midst of expounding on his theory that so-called victimless crimes—such as the selling of drugs, pornography, prostitution, and the like—ought to be decriminalized on the grounds that such activity is voluntary, not coercive in nature and, as such, poses no serious threat to property or innocent individuals. Legalizing such activities, he said, would also defund organized crime and free up law enforcement officials to pursue serious criminals.

But Olson was interrupted by a member of the Christian Right in the audience: "One purpose of government is to provide a role model for people, to set some moral standards. What kind of society would we have if government actually condoned such activity? Do you actually believe, for example, that people ought to be permitted to fornicate in public parks if they want?"

"I, for one, am appalled at the idea of public parks," Olson answered. "The solution to your dilemma, of course, is to get rid of publicly owned lands. Then the question becomes: Should government prevent consenting adults from engaging in a relationship on private property? I think the answer is clearly no."

At another Third Generation meeting, Roy Jones, then a 25-year-old Washington representative of the Moral Majority, which has since changed its name to the Liberty Federation, spoke on "Religion, Moral Issues, and Politics." He pointed out that religious belief played an enormous role in the founding and history of America and that the first settlers sailed to America's shores to escape religious persecution. The Supreme Court's 1962 ruling to outlaw prayer in public schools, said Jones, thus marked a sharp break from the American tradition.

"The American tradition also believes in separation of church and state," asserted a Reagan appointee from the Justice Department. "Government does a terrible job even delivering the mail. Why should we trust it to teach religion?"

"It is the media and other liberal interests that have labeled this the school prayer issue," Jones retorted. "The fact is, it's a free speech issue. What we have now is state-sanctioned religious persecution and discrimination. In some places, students have to hide in hallways to hold a prayer meeting and change location every day so they aren't caught by school officials. Olivia Mendez, an eight-year-old second grader from Sanford, Florida, was disciplined and publicly humiliated in front of her schoolmates at a Christmas party for passing out Christmas cards with the word 'Jesus' on them. I have more than a thousand such cases that are documented and sitting in my office right now."

Grover Norquist, president of Americans for Tax Reform, in his talk on "Building the Conservative Movement for Tomorrow," declared that "personnel is policy." Norquist is called by some the Lenin of the Third Generation, because of his interest in the mechanics of building a political movement and then transforming it into a governing coalition. "Stalin was running the personnel department, while Trotsky was fighting the White Army," Norquist told a standing-room-only crowd. "So, when push came to shove for control of the Soviet Union, Stalin won." With this principle in mind, "conservatives must do all they can to make sure conservatives get jobs in Washington."

For years, liberals have used Social Security as a club with which to flog conservatives. And the issue became a major preoccupation of those at Third Generation discussions. But Peter Ferrara, a Harvard Law School graduate, former senior staffer at the White House Office on Policy Development, and author of three books on the coming Social Security crisis, had some encouraging news for conservatives in his talk, "How the Third Generation Can Cut the Federal Budget in Half and Still Win Elections."

"Even if young people entering the work force today were to receive all the benefits they are promised, it would be a miserable deal for them," he said. "They will be getting zero or negative return on their investment, and could do much better by putting that money in an Individual Retirement Account or Keogh plan." This is good news for believers in the free market, as "the Social Security issue is beginning to cut in a conservative direction," said Ferrara, citing a *Washington Post/* ABC News poll, which found that 74 percent of those under 30 believe they will receive nothing from Social Security when they retire.

Joseph Perkins talked about the "Rising Tide of Conservatism Among Young Black Americans." Perkins's skill as a journalist for the campus newspaper at Howard University so impressed *The Wall Street Journal*'s editor, Robert Bartley, that Bartley hired Perkins immediately after graduation as an editorial writer. In his talk, Perkins said that affirmative action policies are condescending, counterproductive, and contribute to a poor self-image among black Americans. Many young blacks, he said, feel they no longer need affirmative action to compete on an equal footing with whites.

"I can say with confidence that I have never been denied anything I wanted because of the color of my skin," said Perkins. "Liberals do no service to black people by hammering on the notion that blacks can't compete with whites. This demoralizes black people and leads to a defeatist attitude."

"But conservatives have been hurt badly by the civil rights issue," commented one member of the audience. "Liberals seem to have bought the black vote by promoting affirmative action and policies of preferential treatment."

"Conservatives won't win the black vote by copying the liberals," Perkins answered. "We'll win it, eventually, by continuing to present the conservative case, not by waffling on principles we know to be true."

Perkins went on to cite survey data indicating blacks are becoming increasingly conservative in their attitudes, even if this is not yet reflected in their voting habits. Sixty-two percent of blacks, for example, oppose abortion; 52 percent oppose busing; 71 percent favor school prayer. "We need to make it clear to black people that it is conservatives with whom they most agree," said Perkins.

As was the case during the sixties, it is the lean and hungry activists who shape the political agenda. Then, it was Jerry Rubin, Abbie Hoffman, and Bobby Seale who, through their radical approach, focused the country's attention on their issues and drove the political and cultural debate to the Left. Today, the young are still idealistic, but they have seen the failure of the Left's policy prescriptions and, as a result, have moved in the opposite direction.

"I see my role in the movement as helping push the intellectual debate farther and farther right," said Dinesh D'Souza at that first meeting of the Third Generation. "We are not interested in containment of the Soviet menace anymore. We want to roll it back. We are not interested in Mutual Assured Destruction as a way to deter a first-strike attack from the Soviets. We want the capacity to knock their missiles down even after they are launched. We are not interested in government solutions to social problems. Our faith rests with the private sector that expands the economic pie instead of only spreading the existing pie around."

These are just a few examples of the sharp exchanges at Third Generation meetings and the intellectual and ideological fervor of Third Generation members.

"The central mission of the Third Generation," Congressman Jim Courter's chief of staff Mac Carey told the Third Generation audience, "is to continue building the lines of communication between the various interests within our movement and develop a set of signals so that we can all move in one direction, to accomplish a common objective—the rebuilding of America along the principles established by this country's founders."

A major aim of the Third Generation project is to provide a place where religiously motivated conservatives can talk to libertarians, where New Right can meet Old Right, where neoconservatives can meet with people who might agree with them on everything except social issues—and to identify the emerging leadership representing the various political and philosophical camps.

Another feature that appeals to the young audience is that the meetings provide opportunities to meet others of roughly the same age and philosophical stripe. Coors beer, soft drinks, and cheese and crackers are served in the Heritage lobby before the program begins. Afterward, most of the group convenes at a neighboring restaurant where discussions continue well into the evening. Business cards are exchanged, and occasionally couples are formed.

The result seems to be the development in Washington of a young conservative network—both political and social in nature—that is vast in terms of numbers of people involved. While there always will be disagreements in such a large group, Third Generation members appear unified in at least two areas: the dismantling of the liberal welfare state and the rollback of the Soviet empire. In addition, liberalism's open hostility toward religion has brought hundreds of new activists to Washington, who have made prayer in school, the right to life, and choice in education important parts of the conservative agenda.

The name Third Generation was selected to reflect the organic development of American intellectual and political conservatism, which seems to have evolved in three distinct conceptual (though not necessarily biological) generations.

First Generation conservatives were mainly intellectual groundbreakers. They include Friedrich A. Hayek (*Road to Serfdom*), James Burnham (*Suicide of the West*), William F. Buckley, Jr. (*Up from Liberalism*), Russell Kirk (*The Conservative Mind*), Whittaker Chambers (*Witness*), Frank Meyer (*In Defense of Freedom*), Henry Regnery (publisher of many important conservative books), and Frank Hanighen and James Wick who began publishing *Human Events* in 1944. As if to answer Lionel Trilling's 1950 charge that "there are no conservative ideas in general circulation," William F. Buckley, Jr., in 1955 founded the most important journal of conservative opinion, *National Review*. As dramatic, was the rise to prominence of the Hoover Institution on War, Revolution, and Peace at Stanford University. The first major conservative think tank in America, Hoover had only six researchers when Glenn Campbell took over as director in 1960. Today, still under Campbell's leadership, it boasts 70 full-time scholars.

For the First Generation, the watershed year was 1964 when the country saw the first major party nomination of a genuinely conservative presidential candidate in recent history. Though Barry Goldwater lost the election, his campaign spawned the Second Generation of conservative leaders and activists, who had learned from defeat that conservatives needed to organize more effectively if they were to win politically.

The Second Generation designed political strategies, trained candidates, set up political action committees, perfected direct-mail fund raising, brought together a coherent body of politically powerful ideas, and established think tanks to produce books, studies, and reports on public policy. Prominent Second Generation figures and institutions include Paul Weyrich, Edwin Feulner, Jr., Richard Viguerie, Howard Phillips, Norman Podhoretz, Midge Decter, Stan Evans, Irving Kristol, Jerry Falwell, *Wall Street Journal* editor Robert Bartley, The Heritage Foundation, the American Enterprise Institute, The Center for Strategic and International Studies, the National Conservative Political Action Committee various public interest legal foundations, and the periodicals *Commentary* and *The American Spectator*. These individuals, institutions, and publications provided intellectual ammunition for the political battle, built a structure that could circumvent the liberal media, disseminated conservative ideas to the general public, and pressured lawmakers to consider conservative policy proposals.

The Second Generation concentrated largely on attracting new ethnic, religious, and economic groups to the conservative fold—Jews, Catholics, born-again Christians, and blue-collar workers. Many of these were traditionally Democratic voters. No longer was conservatism identified with elitism. It had become more populist and inclusive, a position with which Main Street America could identify.

The first hint of the Second Generation's political strength occurred in 1978, when the Republicans picked up three seats in the Senate and eleven in the House. Then came 1980 and the election of conservative dream candidate Ronald Reagan.

The Third Generation is heir to the successes and momentum built by these groups and individuals. The greatest achievements of the First and Second Generations seem to have been to discredit liberalism intellectually and to contain its political advance. The task of the Third Generation is to begin to "roll back," on all fronts, the liberal conquests of the last half century.

After more than 60 meetings of the Third Generation in The Heritage Foundation's Lehrman Auditorium, it is apparent that tomorrow's conservative leaders will bring to the political and policy struggle advantages not enjoyed by previous generations. Among them:

1) *The Third Generation, in stark contrast to previous generations, is a vast army and can deploy a tremendous number of troops in the battle over government.* Reagan's victory in 1980 brought thousands of young conservatives from around the country into Washington's policy-making establishment.

2) *By giving them jobs in his Administration, Reagan has credentialed hundreds of Third Generation conservative activists for higher level jobs in future administrations.* "They aren't always the most glamorous or exciting positions," says Morton Blackwell who, as a former White House official in the Office of

Public Liaison, made it his special mission to identify young, talented conservatives and find them jobs in the Administration. "But it's the people in these jobs who will head up the agencies and write the policies of tomorrow." Blackwell now heads the Leadership Institute, which organizes training schools for young conservative activists.

3) *The Third Generation is enthusiastic and confident, driven by a sense of purpose that comes with success.* Its members, except for the very oldest, have never experienced, firsthand, serious defeat. Their political consciousness has been shaped not by Lyndon Johnson's crushing Barry Goldwater in 1964, but by the nation's massive repudiation of the Great Society with the back-to-back Reagan landslide election victories of 1980 and 1984. To most young conservatives today, Watergate and the Vietnam War are bizarre and inexplicable chapters from history books.

4) *The liberal opposition appears inept to the Third Generation.* Its members are invigorated when they think back to the dismal days of Jimmy Carter, and they cannot imagine America ever turning back to his policies and way of thinking. Liberalism appears so tired and so intellectually and morally bankrupt that it is difficult for the Third Generation to envision defeat in the long term.

5) *Liberalism, because of its failures, is now on the moral defensive.* Liberalism cannot point to a single socialist, collectivist, or communist success in history. The disaster of economic redistribution is tragically obvious in such countries as Ethiopia and Mozambique; both were food-exporting nations before the communists took over. Today, millions there face starvation. Liberalism's redistributionist policies have also failed in the U.S. George Gilder, Thomas Sowell, and Charles Murray, among others, have confirmed statistically what conservatives have known intuitively for years:

by inducing chronic economic dependency, welfare creates a permanent welfare class, hits black America hardest, dooms the poor to generations of poverty, and devastates the family unit. The conclusion: When we pay for poverty, we get more of it; when we reward production, we see economic growth. The Third Generation now has the luxury of irrefutable and documented proof of the truth of these economic laws.

6) *The Third Generation is on the moral offensive.* Its members have seen, firsthand, the failure of economic redistribution in all its forms. Young conservatives are forcing liberals to account for the millions doomed to poverty at home because of socialist welfare policies and the scores of millions who have died abroad because of liberalism's failure to address the threat of international socialism—or communism. In contrast to liberalism's policy prescriptions, Third Generation conservatives point to free market capitalism as history's most successful economic system.

7) *The new conservatives appear confident, almost cocky at times.* Conservative intellectuals of previous decades were tentative and often apologetic about their philosophical beliefs. The dramatic shift in attitude is evident not only with regard to economic policies, which have been an obvious success, but also in foreign affairs, frequently the Achilles heel of conservatives who in previous years often found themselves defending such authoritarian despots (albeit friendly to the U.S.) as Somoza and the Shah of Iran.

The overarching theme of virtually every meeting of the Third Generation is that liberal foreign policy strategy has caused much misery in the world, while conservative policies have brought a halt to the advance of tyranny. "Between 1973 and 1980, for example, nine countries fell to the Soviet Union. Reagan, by contrast, has not yielded a single inch of free soil to communist rule, and one country, Grenada, has even been liberated from Marxist tyranny," 30-year-old *Policy Review* editor Adam Meyerson told a packed auditorium in his talk, "Reagan's Foreign Policy Revolution." Moreover, Reagan appears to have saved the Philippines and Haiti from the communists and is supporting anti-communist liberation movements around the globe—the Mujahadeen in Afghanistan, Jonas Savimbi in Angola, the contras in Nicaragua, to name a few—as part of an overall policy to roll back Soviet gains made under liberal U.S. administrations. This policy allows Third Generation conservatives to be anti-colonialist, and to support true liberation movements. Liberals, in turn, have backed themselves into the hopeless role of defenders of the status quo, including Soviet-installed colonial regimes. The emergence of anti-communist national liberation movements attempting to evict an outside power—the Soviet Union—has interjected an aura of romance into the defense of Western interests, which appeals to the young and idealistic. Indeed, this theme has been the subject of numerous Third Generation discussions.

8) *Young conservative activists today are eager to govern, representing a dramatic shift in mind-set from that of previous generations.* The First Generation conservatives concerned themselves mainly with broad principles, in part because they were so far from the levers of power. The Second Generation spent most of its energy attacking the existing liberal governing establishment so that conservative candidates might one day gain power. "But we have had difficulty transforming ourselves from an activist political movement into a governing establishment," 29-year-old *National Review* editor Richard Vigilante told a Third Generation audience. "We learned how to be philosophers and activists. But once we gained control of government, we failed to place conservatives in many key positions. Our job in future years is to build a permanent conservative governing infrastructure."

9) *Today's young conservative activist enjoys working in Washington, a city, by its nature, generally antithetical to conservative principles and usually avoided by most older conservatives.* Reagan has had difficulty finding experienced conservatives who will accept appointments to top Administration positions. As a result, many young conservatives in Washington are holding down government posts ordinarily reserved for their seniors. They maintain that, as long as someone must govern, that someone ought to be a conservative.

10) *The Third Generation is increasing its presence in the national media.* Robert Bartley of *The Wall Street Journal,* for example, has brought some of the most talented young conservative journalists onto his editorial page staff, including deputy features editor John Fund, hired at age 26; editorial writer Joseph Perkins, hired at age 25; and Greg Fossedal, also hired at age 25, author of *A Defense that Defends* and a founder of *The Dartmouth Review.* (Fossedal has since moved on to become the media fellow at the Hoover Institution.)

M. Stanton Evans, a 30-year veteran in the battle for conservative principles, a syndicated columnist, and a former newspaper editor, has established the National Journalism Center in Washington, which trains college seniors and recent graduates who have conservative inclinations to become professional journalists. Evans's program is placing dozens of the Center's graduates every year in important positions in the news media across the country.

Other breeding grounds for young conservative writers are *The Washington Times, The Boston Herald, The New York Post, The Detroit News,* and *The San Diego Union.* In 1983, Adam Meyerson, at age 30, took over as editor of *Policy Review,* The Heritage Foundation's quarterly journal.

Many of Meyerson's contributors are under 30. "Some of the best writing in America is being done by conservatives just out of college," Meyerson says.

11) *The sheer number of Third Generation activists, administrators, journalists, policy analysts, and thinkers allows an extremely useful division of labor and specialization.* In the past, all efforts had to be devoted to merely laying down conservatism's broad principles and informing the voting public via direct mail with calls to action. Today the effort is widespread. There are experts who specialize in tax policy, getting the U.S. out of U.N., Health and Human Services, religious issues, or the Strategic Defense Initiative. A number of think tanks now do nothing but promote the privatization concept, a strategy to shift the functions of government to the private sector. Grover Norquist's ad hoc committee, Americans for Tax Reform, devoted itself to promoting President Reagan's tax reform proposal.

A number of organizations concentrate exclusively on lobbying for U.S. aid to Jonas Savimbi's anti-communist national liberation movement (UNITA) in Angola; other groups focus on support for the democratic freedom fighters in Nicaragua; still others encourage a return to the gold standard. The Washington Legal Foundation is a conservative counterpart of the American Civil Liberties Union.

A list of the conservative groups now in existence would fill a small book. Many of them are staffed almost exclusively by members of the Third Generation. These young conservatives will remain in Washington long after the departure of Ronald Reagan, forming an administrative, intellectual, and activist establishment. Before 1980, the conservative movement had neither the resources nor the manpower to support such a vast array of specialized conservative activities.

Third Generation members, then, are numerous, eager, confident, and well-educated in their specific areas of interest. As such, they represent an entirely new conservative breed, perhaps less inclined toward general philosophical speculation than toward winning individual political and policy battles. This development comes at a particularly vulnerable time for liberalism, whose base has begun to deteriorate. It seems, moreover, that America's youngest voters are the most conservative, suggesting that the conservative revolution has not yet reached its full potential in terms of political power. According to Professor Alexander Astin's yearly sampling of 200,000 college freshmen, sponsored by the American Council on Education and conducted by UCLA's Laboratory for Research on Higher Education, dramatic shifts toward conservative or traditional values have occurred since the 1970s. These social trends, combined with the political victories, are generating more and more confidence and enthusiasm among Third Generation conservative leaders and activists and, to borrow a phrase from Lenin, are attracting more and more cadres into the revolution's vanguard.

Before Reagan ascended to the presidency, and even in the initial years of his Administration, the various elements of the conservative movement often moved in disparate directions. The *Human Events* people had little contact with the *Commentary* people. The *Commentary* people rarely talked to *National Review* people, who, in turn, had almost no communication with those fighting in legislative battles on Capitol Hill. There were feuds between traditionalist, libertarian, neo, fundamentalist, and fusionist conservatives. Often, more time seemed to be spent on hairsplitting discussions on issues ranging from doctrinal to personality conflicts than in actually winning political and policy struggles.

Reagan provided the unifying glue that brought these

elements together to achieve victory in 1980. Everyone in the conservative community seems to be able to agree on him—even if they cannot agree on whether he should focus his efforts primarily on tax cuts or slashing the budget, school prayer or education vouchers, strategic defense or better ICBMs.

But what happens to the conservative movement after Reagan? Are there philosophical themes stronger than differences in personality and doctrinal emphasis that can transcend his departure from the political stage and keep the conservative movement heading in generally one direction after 1988? These seem to be the most nagging questions for the Third Generation. A statement by Frank Cannon at the second meeting of the Third Generation in January 1984 captures the attitude that pervades the group: "Ronald Reagan is a transitional president. He helped stop the momentum of 50 years of unchecked liberal policies. That alone was a Herculean task. But the real victories for the conservative revolution lie ahead."

What follows is a sampling of what has been said at Third Generation meetings the group convenes every second Wednesday at 6:00 P.M. in The Heritage Foundation's Lehrman Auditorium. The material is taken both from prepared presentations and, to a lesser extent, from informal comments made by Third Generation members in attendance. It is necessarily an incomplete compilation, covering about half the young speakers who made formal remarks and only a fraction of what was said during the informal discussions. Because the remarks contained in this volume were delivered over a two-year period, we have updated some to take important recent history into account. And we have had to omit much fine material, in most cases because of space, but also because some talks concerned issues of transitory interest or the speaker was promoting a particular candidate or political party. It is, of course, impossible to project on the printed page the energy that permeates every meeting of the Third Generation. The best way to understand why the group has grown from seventeen to some 400 members in two and a half years is to experience the fortnightly event. This anthology attempts to include material that best represents the philosophical and political approach of the group, as well as to introduce some rising young stars and thus provide a preview of the impetus and mentality of the post-Reagan conservative movement.

Benjamin Hart
Director of Lectures and Seminars,
The Heritage Foundation

Chapter One

THE REAGAN REVOLUTION: FACT OR FANTASY?

Through his unprecedented ability to communicate broad conservative themes, Ronald Reagan has moved the entire political debate sharply right. Conservatives have now won the war of ideas on every foreign, domestic, and social policy issue. But President Reagan has failed to place conservatives in key positions in his Administration. As a result, many of his initiatives have not been implemented, and the potential of his Administration has gone unfulfilled. But most Third Generation members are confident that the conservative revolution will continue long after Reagan has left the political stage.

GREGORY FOSSEDAL: Culturally speaking, surf's up in America in the 1980s. The political revolution that has taken place is obvious to anyone who reads GNP figures, the Dow Jones stock average, or the inflation index. But a lot more is happening out there as well.

Outrageousness, for one thing, is back. In the seventies, Americans and the journalists themselves took the press much too seriously. Endless moralizing about this and that covered the pages of our newspapers and filled network news broadcasts. Dave Kingman, the homerun hitter, encapsulated the lighthearted attitude that most Americans today expect from athletes and journalists when he sent a live rat to a reporter who was pestering him.

William "The Refrigerator" Perry, has captured the hearts of Chicago Bears fans with his one-yard touchdown dives and amiable gap-toothed smile. In basketball, millions of Americans applaud the twin towers of Houston, Ralph Sampson and Akeem Alajuwan, the unbelievable ball handling of Earvin "Magic" Johnson, and the greatest player ever, Larry Bird of Boston. It is achievement, not politics, that dominates the athletic arena in the eighties, and these players are reinventing basketball.

Despite negative reviews, millions of people are flooding the theaters to see freedom fighter films, such as *Red Dawn, Rambo, Missing in Action,* and *White Nights.* Movies designed to raise our consciousness are bombing, while people line up for pure entertainment, such as *Back to the Future, Top Gun,* and anything with Rodney Dangerfield, the comic who has everyone laughing.

In business, Horatio Alger types dominate, turning potential into wealth in places like Silicon Valley. No longer is opportunity seen as flowing from a benevolent state. Women and black Americans are starting businesses in record numbers, thanks in part to a pair of radical tax cuts designed to spur private enterprise. Only a few years ago, the supply-side idea was considered kooky and derisively labeled "Reaganomics." Today, Reaganomics is the envy of the world. All of Western Europe and much of Asia are now implementing various tax cut schemes. Even the French socialist Francois Mitterand is cutting taxes. He's become a "born-again" supply-sider. *The New York Times,* which fought Reagan's 1981 tax cuts tooth and nail on its editorial pages, has been promoting further rate reductions because, as one *Times* editorial (Aug. 19, 1986) phrased it, lower tax rates will "increase incentives to work and invest."

Remember when owning your own home was a thing of the past? Today, with the continuing plunge in interest rates, almost everyone can afford one. Record numbers of new houses are being built, and record numbers of people are moving into them.

New York City was a rotting apple in the seventies, bankrupt and disintegrating. Ed Koch, who sported a 100 percent rating from Americans for Democratic Action while in Congress, took over as mayor, slashed spending, announced that there would be no more preferential treatment for minorities, and cracked down severely on crime. New York City has since become a major tourist attraction, and Lady Liberty has received a face lift—from private enterprise, I might add.

San Diego, San Francisco, and Los Angeles pulse with the corpuscles of hardworking immigrants from Latin America and Asia, many of whom fled communist tyranny.

Both *The Washington Post* and the liberal standard-bearer *The New Republic* came out in favor of sending U.S. assistance to the freedom fighters in Nicaragua. What a turnaround from only a few years ago.

Some of the best journalism in America is coming from the college campuses where some 70 conservative student newspapers are now publishing on a regular basis. I helped start one myself back in 1980. This movement is producing a new generation of journalists. Mike Waller of the George Washington *Sequent* and Mike Johns of the *Miami Tribune* were the first student journalists to travel with the freedom fighters of Nicaragua. Charles Bork of Yale has filed frequent dispatches from the front in Afghanistan and has traveled extensively with the Mujahadeen. Grover Norquist of Harvard has made a number of trips to Angola in order to get a firsthand look at Jonas Savimbi's UNITA forces fighting the Cuban-installed Angolan government. These young and talented journalists are rapidly becoming the

Sidney Schanbergs and Seymour Hershes of tomorrow. But instead of covering the march of communism, they are writing about the march of freedom.

The University of Chicago's *Counterpoint*, founded by John Podhoretz, has produced a number of young conservative journalists who are writing about events in the nation's capital. Stan Evans's National Journalism Center in Washington is training and placing young, talented journalists in papers, radio, and television stations across the country every day. Many of them are disposed to causes that advance individual freedom, whether it is liberating territory under communist control, slashing the federal budget, or cutting tax rates. Evans and Novak, with their populist "average man" tone, have become the most influential political commentators in Washington. The brawling writing style and ribald political commentary of R. Emmett Tyrrell's *American Spectator* has people across the country laughing and thinking.

Astride the "roaring eighties," like a colossus, stands the amiable, grandfather president who, like Calvin Coolidge, works a six-hour day, manages to pass radical tax-slashing legislation, and gets hundreds of millions of dollars to freedom fighters even before he finishes breakfast. A radio broadcaster, movie actor, and newspaper columnist, Ronald Wilson Reagan will leave the public stage remembered as this century's greatest president. His message is the same as F. Scott Fitzgerald's, who in the 1920s wrote, "You had the feeling anything could happen, anything at all." In just a few short years, America has returned from the brink and once again become the land of the possible.

FRANK CANNON: Have we seen a Reagan Revolution in America? For a revolution to occur, there must be more than just a change in leaders. By revolution, we mean a fundamental change in assumptions that dominate the culture, a reordering of social priorities, and a radical restructuring of what government does. That a revolution has taken place can be proved by remembering what America looked like in the seventies and comparing that to what we are seeing today.

I remember America leaving Vietnam in disgrace. Freedom was on the defensive both morally and strategically. The image emblazoned on my consciousness was a U.S. helicopter taking off from our embassy grounds in Saigon with desperate people clinging to its runners, vainly trying to climb aboard. We then stood paralyzed as nine countries dropped into the Soviet orbit between 1973 and 1980. The communist tide seemed unstoppable. In 1976, the Congress of the United States cemented the Soviet acquistion of Angola by passing the Clark Amendment, which prohibited American assistance of any kind to the anti-communist forces there. The American Ambassador to the United Nations, Andrew Young, actually called the Cuban presence in Angola "a force for stability." Moreover, we saw an American president spend $132 million in taxpayer money to provide assistance to the Sandinista government. Incredibly, we were subsidizing the establishment of a Marxist-Leninist dictatorship on our continent.

Compare this to American foreign policy in the eighties. We used military force to throw the Cubans out of Grenada, marking the first rollback of communism in history. Americans were then treated to pictures of American medical students rescued from Grenada kissing the ground upon their return to safety and freedom in the United States.

Nor did America remain locked in paralysis in the face of increased Libyan terror. We shot down two of Colonel Qadhafi's planes over the Gulf of Sidra when they challenged our right to free passage in international waters. In retaliation for repeated acts of aggression against Americans, we bombed terrorist training bases in Libya. Not surprisingly, Americans demonstrated strong support for the judicious use of military force by a decisive president.

Throughout the world, anti-communist resistance movements are growing within Soviet-controlled territory. President Reagan has responded with the articulation of a new U.S. foreign policy position. The Reagan Doctrine, as it is now called, seeks not merely to contain Moscow's advances, but to actually roll back Soviet gains.

Following the electoral defeat of liberal Iowa Democrat, Senator Dick Clark, on a wave of conservative sentiment, we saw the subsequent repeal of the Clark Amendment, allowing U.S. aid to flow to UNITA, the anti-communist, pro-Western movement fighting for democracy in Angola. The repeal of both Clark's tenure in office and his amendment marked the repeal of the "blame America first" syndrome of the 1970s.

This was followed by the House voting to provide overt assistance to the anti-communist freedom fighters in Nicaragua. It would seem that democracy is once again on the moral and strategic offensive.

Conservatives are winning the war of ideas even on the issue of nuclear weapons. Conservatives have taken the moral high ground by promoting a concept of strategic defense, which offers a way out of the balance of terror without resorting to unilateral disarmament. Nuclear freeze resolutions have become irrelevant. Despite the derisive tag of "Star Wars" placed on the Strategic Defense Initiative by liberal detractors, virtually every week sees a new technological breakthrough bringing SDI closer to reality.

The contrast between the seventies and the eighties is just as apparent on the economic front. In the post-Watergate era, wage and price controls were the Republican alternative to Democratic stagflation. Concern in the seventies centered around shrinking resources. That decade's vision of society was characterized in books with such titles as *Spaceship Earth, Limits to Growth,* and *The Zero Sum Society.*

Jimmy Carter, perhaps more than anyone, encapsulated the thinking of the period with his Administration's Global 2000 report. "If present trends continue," said the Carter study, "the world in 2000 will be more crowded, more polluted, less stable ecologically. Barring revolutionary advances in technology, life for more people on earth will be more precarious in 2000 than it is now unless the nations of the world act decisively to alter current trends."

Carter did act decisively, giving us more government intervention, more regulation, more taxes, more belt-tightening, more austerity, and a ravaged economy, making the Global 2000 report a self-fulfilling prophecy.

President Reagan, in strong contrast, called for a limit to the growth of government as he sought to unleash the productive capacity of the American people. The Reagan plan involved less government intervention, less regulation, less taxation, less belt-tightening, and less austerity. In a direct refutation of liberal predictions, the result of Reagan's policies has been more food, a cleaner environment, more safety, tremendous technological advances, less poverty, and more prosperity.

Conservatives know that government, through taxation, bureaucracy, and endless red tape, is a roadblock that inhibits progress, creates shortages, and prevents new technological breakthroughs. Reagan understands that individuals are the engines of progress; individuals create surpluses; and individuals make new discoveries that benefit everyone.

By the end of his eight years in office, Reagan will have cut top tax rates about 60 percent. Slowly, people in both parties are beginning to understand that more government was not the solution to our economic woes of the seventies. Deregulation of oil and airlines has produced great benefits for the consumer. Inflation and interest rates have been slashed to pre-Carter levels.

During the 1970s, liberal social policy was advanced primarily through the federal court system. The Supreme Court, along with other federal courts, extended beyond all reason the rights of the criminally accused, continued to prevent prayer in the schools, promoted special rights for homosexuals, and condoned pornography under the guise of First Amendment protection.

To many, including myself, the height of this judicial activism on behalf of liberal causes was the 1973 *Roe v. Wade* decision legalizing abortion. Remarkably, five of seven judges who gave legal cover to the violent slaughter of millions of unborn babies were appointed by Republican presidents.

Under the Reagan Presidency, conservatives have succeeded in blocking the two primary legislative initiatives proposed by the feminist movement: the Equal Rights Amendment and comparable worth. Conservatives have scored modest gains in limiting the federal government's role in subsidizing abortions and in allowing the meetings of religious groups access to schoolrooms on the same basis as other extracurricular activities.

Millions of Christian activists have entered the political process in recent years, many primarily motivated by the issues that revolve around family and community. These people have influenced government at all levels. Their impact in making party organs, local governments, national candidates, and even the media more aware of the importance of social issues cannot be overstated.

What I see as the most important single development of the Reagan Presidency is the replacement of hundreds of liberal judges by conservative jurists. This will have a profound effect on the entire policy spectrum, but it will be felt most acutely in the area of social issues. William Rehnquist, the dissenter of the seventies, has become Chief Justice in the eighties. Soon his views may well be in the majority. The ferocity of the liberal attacks against Rehnquist's nomination only serves to underscore the tremendous importance of controlling this vital institution of government.

In 1980, when Ronald Reagan ran for president, he was attacked by the liberal establishment as an extremist, who would plunge the country into war, cause a depression, throw elderly widows out into the street, rekindle racism, turn back the clock on progress. Today, he is the most popular president of modern times, and this is not because of his acting ability. It is because of his policies.

The conservative vision of Ronald Reagan has fundamentally changed the policy debate in this country. His philosophy of government has emerged victorious over liberalism in the war of ideas. This is what is meant by the Reagan Revolution.

But a revolution in ideas is not enough. Reagan's conservative policies, when implemented, have been enormously successful, as we all knew they would be. But if there has been a failure in his Administration—and I believe there has—it is in the area of personnel. The maxim, "personnel is policy," conservatives have come to understand well. Without conservatives in government positions —and I mean every government position from Secretary of State to elevator operators—we will not see the implementation of a conservative agenda.

Important pockets of resistance to President Reagan's policy initiatives, even within his own Administration, continue to undermine his policies. The tragedy is that many of these betrayers of the Reagan Revolution are the President's own appointments. Because Reagan has not been scrupulous about appointing people who hold his philosophy, his Administration has fallen far short of its potential.

Ben Hart, in his ripping analysis of U.S. foreign policy entitled "Rhetoric Versus Reality: How the State Department Betrays the Reagan Vision," presents a comprehensive bill of particulars. His indictments include failure of the U.S. State Department to push adequately for U.S. assistance to anti-communist democratic movements in Afghanistan, Africa, Central America, and Asia. Hart places the blame squarely on the shoulders of the President's own foreign policy advisors. The State Department continues to exist beyond the reach of any Reagan Revolution.

Outside Reagan's own Administration, the picture is even more bleak. The Democrat-controlled House of Representatives remains trapped in the George McGovern mind-set, even after two landslide electoral mandates for conservative change. Conservatives have made little headway in that critical governing institution. Frank Gregorsky in his study, "What's Wrong with Democratic Foreign Policy," published by The Republican Study Committee, shows a Democratic House leadership incapable of condemning atrocities committed by communists, while holding America accountable for virtually all international conflicts. The intransigence of this leadership produced a mammoth struggle to provide even token assistance to the freedom fighters of Nicaragua, despite the clear record of Sandinista totalitarian repression.

More important, the President's revolutionary Strategic Defense Initiative, which can provide permanent protection against a Soviet first-strike missile attack, is dangerously close to being betrayed. Again, we see the institutional resistance to full and proper funding on the part of Congress. The culprits are members of both parties. In addition, there is talk of sacrificing SDI on the altar of arms control. It is not only the media, but certain elements of Reagan's own White House staff and Administration who are pressing for an arms control agreement with the Soviets, even if it means giving up our shield against a Kremlin missile attack. It is personnel in the key committees of Congress, within the Defense and State Department arms control bureaucracies, and even inside the White House, who threaten to snatch defeat from the jaws of victory.

It almost goes without saying that the strongest bulwark against conservative change is the media. Numerous studies have shown this body of unelected policy makers to be totally out of step with the thinking of the American people. Yet each day the voting public is treated to a visual and written assault from a group of people who say, outright, that they are allies of the Left. Because the media have a direct effect on policy, I would classify them as a critical institution of the ruling establishment and one that must not be surrendered to the Left.

Changing the U.S. House of Representatives and creating philosophical balance in the media cannot be achieved overnight. But the conservative movement must develop strategies that focus on personnel at all levels of the bureaucracy, the legislative branch, and the media, who play a role in forming policy. A revolution in ideas is not enough. The battle is also over control of the institutions of government. This war is waged every day in Washington and around the country, and conservatives are losing far too many of those skirmishes. The challenge for the Third Generation is not to consolidate conservative gains but to press forward and capture those institutions that still remain in the hands of liberals and still exert enormous influence over policy.

It is only when we begin to win both the battle of ideas and the battle of personnel that we can lay full claim to a conservative revolution.

Richard Brookhiser: The future will depend entirely on whether conservatives or Republicans prevail in setting the agenda. Republicans, by my definition, are people whose consciousness was shaped earlier than ours was. Republicans who are now 50 or 60 years old grew up in a very hostile world. Of Barry Goldwater they used to say: "In your heart, you know he's right." But actually, Republicans thought that most people, in their hearts, knew he was wrong. They never expected to win, because they did not think people would ever be persuaded by their arguments.

This is why Republicans always sit on leads. That is what Nixon always did. He was always shocked by his lead. The campaign strategy was always to do nothing and sit tight or something bad might happen. He never knew why he had a lead. He did not believe it when he had it. He had a gut feeling that everyone hated him and would vote for his opponent if they thought about it for two seconds. Nixon's strategy always was to hunker down and pray that the election would come quickly. That was the Republican psychology.

Republican House Minority Leader Bob Michel's speech at the 1984 Dallas convention was telling. He told us about how he started out in Republican Party politics selling sunflowers for Alf Landon. Now, there is something admirable about that. He had a kind of Jacobite fidelity to a lost cause. If you begin your political life as a boy passing out sunflowers for Alf Landon, you grow up thinking the world is not going to be kind to you. This is something you anticipate.

There are still a lot of these people around. They are good people, well-meaning, but they think we are going to lose, and that Republicans can win only by putting one over on people. That is what Nixon thought. That is what a lot of Republicans still think. I believe the fight for the soul of the party will hinge on the difference between the Republican psychology of losing and the modern conservative pyschology of winning.

Is George Bush more of a conservative or more of a Republican? Which strain in his character will predominate? Who is the conservative champion: Jack Kemp, Bill Armstrong, Pete DuPont, Pat Robertson? If Bush falters, where does the conservative sentiment go? These are all questions we have put on the back burner because Reagan has been so successful. He pleases everyone. But the differences between conservatives and Republicans in approach, psychology, and style will come out when he leaves office.

I have no idea how these differences will be resolved. But I would like to conclude with a note of caution. I do not for a minute believe the notion that many supply-siders and New Right leaders have been promoting lately that the electorate never errs. Jude Wanniski, Jeff Bell, Richard Viguerie, and others tend to deify the opinion of "The People." The People are always right. The good guys win and the bad guys lose in democratic societies. That is silly. People do make mistakes. People often do not see what the important issues are. I think that the people want what is best. They are looking for answers. But I think it is absurd that they will always be right. So just because we are right, does not mean we are necessarily going to win—even if we win the argument.

I do, however, think that the political landscape looks very good for conservative victories in the future. The analyses offered in *The Emerging Republican Majority* by Kevin Phillips and *The Making of the New Majority Party* by William Rusher, published during the Nixon days, were completely on target. Although many of their specific predictions were wrong, history has shown the Phillips and Rusher theses to be substantially correct.

What they said was that over the years the Democratic

Party is peeling off socially conservative Democrats who can be picked up by non-Democratic conservative politicians. That is what they were saying, and it is indisputable that they were right.

In some ways, the best example of this was the one year that Democrats succeeded in getting some of those socially conservative Democrats back. That was in 1976, when Jimmy Carter won his Party's nomination. He was a born-again Christian, a Southerner, a farmer. He had been in the Navy, and he said he was "personally opposed" to abortion. The right-to-life movement had not yet figured out that being personally opposed meant nothing. Moreover, Carter was running against a Republican opponent who was incapable of challenging him for the conservative Democratic constituency. Gerald Ford was not able to force Carter to focus on his issues. Carter sounded good. He sounded conservative, and he got away with it.

Kevin Phillips did an analysis after the 1976 election. He looked at 20 counties in the U.S. that had registered the greatest shift from Nixon in 1972 to Carter in 1976. He found that there was an arc that went from rural New Jersey down to East Texas. These towns were white, rural, middle-class and lower middle-class, and socially very conservative. They abandoned Ford in droves. It turned out, though, that Carter could not turn the trick twice. So these counties came back to Reagan in 1980, and they stayed with him through 1984. What we have seen is Republicans picking up conservative Democrats, who have been abandoned by the Democratic establishment.

But there is another factor, crucial to conservative success, which Terry Teachout wrote about recently in *National Review* in an article on Whittaker Chambers. Teachout made a very interesting point, which I had never heard put quite this way. He refers to a letter Chambers wrote to Bill Buckley back in the 1950s. Chambers was feeling gloomy about the fate of Western civilization, as he usually did. He said there was no hope for conservatism, because conservatism feels a moral obligation to be faithful to the truth. Conservatives can't win in politics because they don't offer anything to the masses. Chambers said it will take a Republican Left to change this gloomy forecast. Now, this sounds even more depressing to me. Who wants Lowell Weicker as the conservative standard-bearer?

But Teachout says that Chambers was wrong in calling it a Republican Left. He did not anticipate a candidate like Reagan, who offered something to the masses. That was tax cuts. The Republicans, at last, had found something attractive to say. Reagan had an idea that appealed to everyone except the most ideological liberals. For that, Ronald Reagan can thank Jack Kemp. And Kemp can thank Irving Kristol, Arthur Laffer, George Gilder, Jude Wanniski, and the other supply-siders. I think this repackaging of conservative economic principles was absolutely essential. We had good arguments. But we finally figured out how to present our case to the masses. We gave them something for voting conservative. We gave them lower taxes.

JOHN BARNES: The major news media, much as they would like us to think otherwise, are a pillar of the national establishment. They are one of the last areas to reflect a major social revolution, such as the advent of the first genuinely conservative president since the 1920s. They have been lagging about five years behind the rest of the country and are only now beginning to perceive the major change wrought by the Reagan Revolution on the American political landscape.

Liberal media bias has been a consistent conservative theme at least since 1952, when the liberal Republican *New York Herald-Tribune* unabashedly used its influence to deny the GOP presidential nomination to conservative favorite

Senator Robert Taft, and to hand it to General Dwight Eisenhower. To a very real extent the national news media, the big city newspapers, the three broadcast networks, *Time, Newsweek,* and so on, reflect the prevailing liberal consensus among America's intellectual elite: liberal-welfarist on domestic policy and generally soft on foreign policy.

Nevertheless, I believe the time has come when we can say with confidence that conservatives are no longer being shut out of the media. Indeed, some liberal critics say the situation has moved altogether in the other direction. That is probably an exaggeration, but there can be no question that conservatives are better represented in the major news media than they were even five years ago.

While many conservatives are critical of some aspects of his thinking, George Will has become probably the leading commentator on public affairs in the country today, through both his columns and his appearances on ABC news. He also collected journalism's highest honor, the Pulitzer Prize, a mere three years after his column first appeared.

For the populist inclined, the Evans and Novak column is nearly as influential as Will's. Former Nixon aide John McLaughlin hosts what is arguably the most popular program on public affairs in the country: *The McLaughlin Group,* which appears on 150 public and two commercial television stations and has vaulted past the more liberal *Agronsky and Company* in popularity. Rare today are the op-ed pages and new TV programs that do not give some voice to conservatives and their ideas.

To a very large extent, conservatives have had as their ally one of their own ideas: the free market and its corollary, high technology. Entrepreneurship and technology have allowed Cable News Network to move into a position as a genuine competitor to the three establishment networks. CNN's *Evans and Novak Show* and *Crossfire* are two of the most popular programs on cable television. New public affairs channels are also becoming available for the airing of conservative opinions.

Satellite transmission has given birth to newspapers such as *USA Today* with its flamboyantly patriotic headlines and chauvinistic approach to the news. *The Washington Times* has launched *Insight*, a conservative national news magazine, and *The Wall Street Journal*, with its unparalleled editorial page, is available coast-to-coast as well as in Europe and Asia.

The arrival in this country of Rupert Murdoch has given full throat to conservative opinions through his newspapers in New York, Boston, and San Antonio. While many "respectable" journalists disdain Murdoch's two-fisted brand of reporting, the fact remains that he is an authentic capitalist willing to put his money where his ideas are, a quality all too rare in the business world. Now that he has begun buying major television stations in an effort to create another network, more of these ideas can expect to find their way onto the airways.

Conservatives have won other victories. In a commercial for his NBC Nightly News, Tom Brokaw is shown emphasizing the efforts his staff goes through to avoid bias. A few years ago it would not have occurred to anyone in the news business to issue such a disclaimer. Columnist M. Stanton Evans continues to place graduates of his National Journalism School in the major media.

It is perhaps an overstatement to say that the Reagan revolution has penetrated the media. Liberal bias still is frequently found in the news coverage. But there has been a recognition, certainly, that conservatives are out there and to be reckoned with. And that is no small achievement.

PATRICK MCGUIGAN: President Reagan may someday be viewed as the John the Baptist of the new America. That is, he hasn't yet made America conservative, but he is a forerunner of things to come—a kind of prophet. Under Reagan we have only made a start at curbing the burden of taxation, and we have barely scratched the surface of runaway federal spending. We have liberated Grenada, but we continue to prop up the Soviet-backed Mozambique regime (with direct aid) and the Warsaw Pact with trade supports.

But Reagan articulates the conservative vision better than any major politician in U.S. history. His weakness is that his easygoing disposition and nonthreatening persona have become the governing style of his Administration. Reagan is what he is: a good man, a great leader in his own way, a man who, if everything had gone perfectly, could have radically changed the course of human history but who instead has laid the basis for the reordering of the American political reality. The actual reordering, though, will have to await a future conservative president.

Chapter Two

WHY CONSERVATIVE IDEAS SHOULD ATTRACT BLACK AMERICANS

Joseph Perkins, Deroy Murdock, and William Keyes argue that not only have black Americans been helped most by conservative, rather than liberal, policies, but that blacks also tend to hold conservative values. Tragically, conservatives have failed to capitalize on this, and, as a result, black America continues to vote overwhelmingly liberal and against the party of Lincoln.

JOSEPH PERKINS: I believe that there is a rising tide of conservatism among young blacks. I also believe that this development will be borne out in the next two presidential elections. Contrary to myths promulgated in the press, blacks by and large are quite conservative on a range of issues. Various surveys substantiate this.

A 1984 National Opinion Research Center sampling, for example, indicated that 62 percent of blacks oppose abortion. A 1983 Associated Press poll showed that 52 percent of blacks oppose busing. And a 1984 Gallup Poll revealed that 71 percent of blacks favor school prayer. Other recent survey data mirror these conclusions.

The question then is why do blacks, who would seem to have conservative instincts, overwhelmingly back liberal candidates. I am not exactly sure of the answer, but I have observed what I think is a philosophical rift between blacks reared before and during the years of the civil rights movement, and those who came afterward. Blacks who have firsthand memory of the civil rights movement have a difficult time discarding the baggage of the past.

During the years of civil rights activism, blacks learned to mau mau guilt-ridden social and political institutions. This created an ethos that they could get what they wanted simply by shouting loud enough without doing much to earn it. Individual initiative and hard work were discounted in favor of charges of racism and discrimination.

But I think black attitudes are changing. As the memory of the civil rights movement recedes, it becomes easier for young blacks to scrutinize the movement and its consequences objectively. This creates a political dialectic, the first signs of which I have already seen. I am convinced that this dialectic will inevitably lead young blacks to conservative beliefs.

Young, college-educated blacks are ripe for a conservative appeal. Unlike their counterparts in the sixties and seventies, most are making it through their four years of college without much campus unrest. And if they are fortunate enough to go to a school that offers a rigorous curriculum that stimulates their intellectual curiosity, they will surely challenge the liberal orthodoxy.

Now, consider young, well-educated, married blacks. Their incomes are, on average, 101 percent of their white counterparts, according to Census Bureau data. Even if this group of upscale blacks tilts toward liberalism, it is difficult for them to argue that vestigial racism has seriously hampered them in life. At some point, they must note the differences in their way of life and that of blacks of the underclass. They must ask themselves something I have asked myself many times: What accounts for my relative success in society, and what accounts for other blacks' failure? Is racism at work? And if it is, as many liberals claim, why am I not a failure, too? Intellectual curiosity will sooner or later prompt an intelligent young black American to ask these questions.

He or she must also wonder why there are so many more black poor in the United States today than there were 20 years ago, despite the billions of dollars poured into poverty programs. Clearly, dollars alone will not alleviate poverty, a fact that requires policy-makers to rethink the issue. New ideas are needed.

But liberals no longer seem to be interested in the war on poverty. They seem more interested in preserving failed programs, while resisting all attempts to replace them with something that might actually work, or at least help, such as enterprise zones, a subminimum wage for black teenagers (so they can get job experience), education vouchers for disadvantaged inner-city youth. These are ideas that seek to address the real problems that face black America—ideas put forth by conservatives. Conservatives know that they must address the problems of the inner city, and they have—while liberals stopped thinking about these problems twenty years ago.

The liberal coalition has become a mish-mash of militant groups, angry with and alienated from mainstream America, which includes mainstream black America. This is why I think future generations of black Americans are going to look more and more to conservatives for answers.

Many liberals might regard my next assertion with skepticism, but I can say in all honesty that I cannot recall a single instance in my entire life when I was denied something by virtue of my race. I do not mean to say that there is no racial discrimination anywhere to be found. I only mean to say that most of my black contemporaries do not blame discrimination every time they suffer a setback. If we accept the premise that racial discrimination today is much less prevalent than in decades past, we are required to place more emphasis on individual initiative and achievement.

Liberals, of course, do not like that. As I see it, they want blacks to be enslaved to the welfare state, grateful to them for their seemingly benevolent largesse. The liberals have a stake in keeping blacks mired in poverty and reliant on welfare because it ensures them a beholden constituency. But this welfare dependency has had devastating effects on black families. It dooms them not to temporary hardship, but to generations of impoverishment.

As for the idea that blacks should be given preferential treatment in jobs, college admissions, and so on because of past racial discrimination, I ask: What about blacks like me, who have never known racial discrimination? It is simply not fair to offer preferential treatement to someone like myself, and other blacks like me, who are in no way victims of racial discrimination.

If you read the sports pages, you know that black golfer Calvin Peete captured the Tournament Players Championship with a record score of 14 under par. For his efforts, he won $162,000. Now, consider what golf would be like if it were subject to affirmative action guidelines. An argument could be made, given the assumptions that govern affirmative action, that black golfers have not, historically, done well at golf. It is a sport dominated by whites. In fact, one reason blacks have not done well is that not so long ago they were prevented from joining most of the good country clubs.

To make up for this injustice, the government would mandate that black golfers like Peete be permitted to play only 15 holes instead of the usual 18. But, of course, this is ridiculous. All Peete required was equal opportunity to become a good golfer. His own skill and determination produced the results.

Peete is fortunate that no one wonders if he succeeded because of preferential treatment. Most black achievers must wonder whether their accomplishments are tainted by affirmative action preference. That is why it is imperative that conservatives—both black and white—impress upon blacks the pernicious consequences of buying into the liberal ethos. It has provided only stigmatizing racial preferences, a degrading welfare system, and a failed War on Poverty. We must persuade blacks that only by inculcating traditional conservative values will they truly join the mainstream of America.

DEROY MURDOCK: "I wish you only failure and obscurity, because voices like yours must be quieted," read the note I received in the mail from A. J. Onofri of Washington, D.C. A few days later, a black man who had read about my political views told me I should "stand in a pot of piss."

As a young American who happens to be black, conservative, and vocal about his beliefs, I have fallen victim to charges of "selling out" to white America and being a "traitor" to my race. While these accusations are most frustrating, they are also puzzling. It seems that blacks are the only citizens in this country who are expected not to disagree with one another.

Debate among other ethnic groups in the U.S. is utterly routine. While the majority of Irishmen voted for Ronald Reagan for president, no one accused former House Speaker Tip O'Neill of "selling out" the Irish. Neoconservative Irving Kristol and New York Mayor Ed Koch can disagree without anyone questioning either's Jewish credentials. Governor Mario Cuomo serves the people of New York with a set of beliefs that conflict with those of New York's junior senator, Alphonse D'Amato. Will the real Italian please stand up?

Just as this diversity of opinion within white ethnic

groups raises no eyebrows, disagreements within other minority groups are starting to look run-of-the-mill. For instance, while long-time Democrat Cesar Chavez organizes farm workers in California, former White House aide Linda Chavez runs in Maryland as the Republican nominee for the U.S. Senate. Mrs. Chavez's candidacy has been hailed as a milestone in Hispanic progress and not denounced as a cynical betrayal of all Mr. Chavez stands for.

Why, then, is political pluralism, one of America's greatest strengths, so strongly discouraged in the black community? Many white liberals, and liberal black leaders, seem to think there is only one black point of view—to which all blacks must subscribe. But given the diversity of backgrounds, values, and ambitions among blacks, the expectation that blacks will hold one set of beliefs is as ludicrous as the idea of unanimous white opinion on any matter.

There is a frightening premise underlying this thinking, which is that blacks are not yet sufficiently sophisticated to disagree with each other or that the black rank and file is not equipped to choose between the differing opinions advocated by blacks of various political complexions.

But the fact is, blacks are becoming increasingly sophisticated in many areas, and, consequently, are being accepted now more than ever before. In politics, William Gray, the Democratic congressman from Pennsylvania, has received kudos for his work as chairman of the House Budget Committee. Washington, Atlanta, Los Angeles, Chicago, Detroit, and Philadelphia are among the many cities that have elected black mayors. Bill Cosby, Eddie Murphy, Whoopi Goldberg, and Lionel Richie are just a few of the performers who have attracted white as well as black audiences. And, with much less fanfare, a black middle class is emerging.

Despite these encouraging signs, the need for debate among blacks has never been greater. While some 55 percent of black infants are born out of wedlock and the number one cause of death among black males between the ages of 18 and 25 is murder, black conservatives cannot accept the notion that the antidotes prescribed by the liberal black leadership are either effective or desirable. With these and other grim realities facing blacks in the United States, it is time to examine alternatives to the liberal welfare state, which, far from curing poverty, seems instead to have created a permanent black underclass.

It is time to stop pushing for government handouts and begin looking to the private sector as the source of opportunity for black Americans. The enterprise zone concept, using tax incentives to draw commerce to inner-city areas, and thus creating jobs, deserves a chance.

Because there is an unemployment rate of about 45 percent among black teenagers, it is time for blacks to look at what the minimum wage has really done for young blacks. It has frozen them out of the job market. It seems self-evident that it is better to be employed at $2.75 an hour than not to be employed because not all employers can afford to pay the minimum wage of $3.35. Reducing the minimum wage for youth in areas of high employment would allow more teenagers to acquire the experience that a first job provides. Before anyone can move up the economic ladder, he must have the chance to stand on the first rung.

It is clear now that public housing has been disastrous for black communities. People do not take pride in something they do not own. Consequently, public housing projects are not treated with respect, but often are plagued by broken windows, scattered garbage, and graffiti. Conservatives have advocated selling these public accommodations to the tenants at reduced prices. The longer people have lived in a housing project, the lower the purchase price should be. People in some areas could be given their homes outright, allowing them either to continue to live in them as owners with the opportunity to make improvements as they saw fit or to sell them, presumably at a profit, and move to other neighborhoods if they chose. This would not only improve the lives of blacks in public housing, it would get the government out of the housing business, thus helping to cut the cost of government.

A similar plan might be put into effect in education. Instead of forcing black children to endure an inferior education in inner-city public schools, the government could give poor, inner-city kids education vouchers allowing them to attend a school of their choice—perhaps a private school in the suburbs. There would then be no need for forced integration, as schools would become naturally integrated as everyone chose the better schools. Meanwhile, inferior schools would fold, since no one would be compelled by law to attend them anymore.

Politics and public policy, it seems to me, ought to be guided by merit, not pigment. The ultimate objective of black America should be a colorblind society, free of quotas and racial preference schemes. This was the dream of Martin Luther King.

Blacks have made a catastrophic error in wedding themselves to one political party. Because they can count on 90 percent of the black vote, Democrats now take blacks for granted. Jesse Jackson was virtually ignored by the Democratic power structure once Walter Mondale wrapped up the 1984 nomination. Once he was no longer a factor, the Democrats excluded Jackson and rapidly distanced themselves from his campaign. Jesse Jackson surrendered to liberalism in order to become a player in Democratic Party politics. He was once a committed pro-life campaigner. His message to blacks used to be that they had to be self-reliant, that achievement should be rewarded, that individual initiative would raise black America out of the abyss of poverty

—not government welfare programs, which create an entire class of helpless dependents. But then Jackson decided that, instead of leading black America, he would become a Democratic Party hack. As a result, he lost credibility. White people treat him as something of a joke, someone not worth listening to. I predict that soon blacks as well will stop listening to Jackson. They will see that it is people like him, not people like me, who have sold out black America by proclaiming liberalism to be their great hope when, in fact, it is liberalism that has caused most of the problems that black America faces today.

Blacks need to look at both parties. Only then will people listen to them. Hispanics, for example, remain uncommitted, and as a result both parties court them, appointing them to office and supporting their efforts. Black Americans, too, can benefit from the political leverage inherent in the bipartisan spirit Hispanics have embraced.

It is time for black America to rid itself of monolithic thinking and instead begin an internal debate. Irishmen, Italians, Jews, and other previously downtrodden ethnic groups brought themselves up partly through the same political give-and-take blacks need today. If black progress is to come from within, black America must have the courage to discuss new views and listen to other voices.

The institutions that will provide lasting wealth and opportunity for black America, in general, are private, particularly the ones started by blacks themselves. We are correct to demand a level playing field, to demand that discriminatory laws be stricken down. We are correct to launch lawsuits against institutions that practice discrimination or that are inherently unfair to blacks. But we are wrong to demand anything more than equal treatment under the law.

Personally, I think it is condescending, and indeed racist, to suggest that blacks need special legal privileges, a kind of head start in order to succeed in a white world. While quotas, goals, timetables, and other forms of affirmative action claim to have blacks' best interests at heart, these efforts actually harm blacks by undermining their sense of self-worth. They also hurt blacks who do not need preferential treatment in order to succeed.

It is not difficult to imagine someone hesitating before allowing a black surgeon to operate on him. He would worry that perhaps the doctor got into medical school on some quota or affirmative action scheme. Now, he might very well not have. But who can really know? The point is, affirmative action hurts the qualified black surgeon. The same quotas that might cause people to challenge the qualified surgeon's credentials might have permitted an unqualified physician to enter medicine.

Blacks should be up in arms over the condescending attitude exhibited by liberals. They should recognize that all liberal programs are based on the theory that blacks are incapable of competing. It is this attitude that has done the most damage to black America.

Now, it is true that conservatives, in general, do not spend all their time thinking about the plight of black Americans. They are generally concerned with their own affairs, running their own businesses and families. That may be the policy black America needs. Maybe, if we were just left alone, we would do just fine. Did anyone ever think of that? Maybe blacks do not need Big Brother looking after them all the time.

But for people to start giving us the dignity we deserve we must stop behaving like helpless dependents. This means looking to the party that is not going to coddle us but instead will free us from the chains of state dependency, which is just another, albeit softer, form of slavery.

Conservatives are not racists. But they are frustrated by the hatred blacks exhibit toward them. If blacks begin to open their minds, if they begin to show the slightest interest in the conservative message of equality under law for all, if blacks, in short, begin to look closely at conservative policy proposals and candidates, you will see conservatives bend over backwards for black support.

Indeed, this is already happening. The opportunities for young blacks in conservative politics are unparalleled. Conservatives are so tired of being labeled racist that today they are sometimes guilty of violating their own principles and giving conservative blacks a boost at the expense of others. So even if only for opportunistic reasons, it behooves young blacks to look in the conservative direction, for the conservative movement is welcoming blacks with open arms. Liberal blacks are a dime a dozen, while conservative blacks are rare, though steadily increasing in number.

Now, of course, opportunism is not a good reason to be a conservative. But it is better than not being a conservative at all. The point I am trying to make is that blacks should look more to conservatives for answers, since liberal principles clearly have failed them. The fundamental principle of modern conservatism answers blacks' initial demand—the demand for equality under the law, not a guarantee of equality of result.

If blacks are to make progress, they must demonstrate independence of mind and not follow liberal leaders like a pack of sheep. It is time to stop behaving like a beleaguered tribe in a foreign land and begin acting like free, patriotic Americans who love their country as much, if not more, than do whites. Only then will political leaders begin to take black opinion seriously.

WILLIAM KEYES: One reason I am involved in conservative politics is that I am particularly concerned about the progress of black America. If blacks are going to progress, it will be because of conservative principles. And if conservative principles are going to be implemented in policy, it will be because we have brought more blacks into the movement.

Conservatives are not doing a very good job at attracting blacks to their cause. The question is: How do we turn this situation around?

The primary reason conservatives have had a problem attracting black support is that they have failed to stand up and make it abundantly clear that it is with the conservatives, not the liberals, that blacks agree on most issues. Consider abortion as one example. In spite of the fact that on Capitol Hill every member of the Congressional Black Caucus advocates and votes for more and more funding for abortion, that sentiment does not reflect the feelings of black people across the country. In fact, a recent survey by the National Opinion Research Center found that 62 percent of blacks are opposed to abortion.

So why do the conservatives not write columns, op-eds, and articles for publications that are widely read by blacks? Why is it that conservatives do not go out and speak in the churches and other public forums in black communities to point out that it is with the conservatives they agree and not the liberals? I believe that conservative candidates should address the congregations of black churches on the issue of right to life.

The same argument holds true for busing, school prayer, and many other issues. On school prayer, in fact, blacks are the single most supportive group. Conservatives do not get the black support they should because they have failed to make it absolutely clear that blacks agree with them.

In February of 1984, when we were considering the President's school prayer initiative, ex-football star Roosevelt Grier, former Harlem Globetrotter Meadowlark Lemon, and former all-pro running back for the Baltimore Colts Lenny Moore, testified before the House Republican Study

Committee in support of school prayer. Rosey Grier was a longtime Democrat, a liberal Democrat, and a friend of the Kennedys. But the school prayer issue moved him from the liberal to the conservative camp. That fall, Black PAC, the group I head, arranged for Rosey to campaign on behalf of President Reagan, Senator Jesse Helms, and several other conservative candidates around the country. This demonstrates what a single issue can do, especially if it is a moral issue.

A second reason conservatives do poorly among blacks is that they do not emphasize that liberal programs have failed to solve the critical problems blacks face.

When I was on the staff of the Joint Economic Committee a few years ago, we conducted a field hearing in Los Angeles. A gentleman named James Kendricks testified that when he ran the CETA [Comprehensive Employment and Training Act] program back in the seventies, he saw that the guidelines set by the Labor Department could lead only to failure. So he decided to disregard the Labor Department's guidelines and do it his own way.

As the trainees were ex-convicts with little job experience, he ignored the Labor Department's directive to teach them how to write resumes and go on interviews. Instead, he taught them how to be productive.

Kendricks taught them the essentials of running a food cooperative—how to go to the market at four o'clock in the morning to get the pick of fresh produce, how to price and sell the food, and how to manage the overall operation.

More important, he promised that everything they earned beyond the cost of operating the co-op would be profit, to be divided equally among the trainees. In other words, he introduced the profit motive, the incentive necessary for them to work hard and succeed. Their business started small, using a shoe box to hold the money and crates full of ice to keep the produce fresh.

But they did so well that they were able to throw away their shoe box and buy a real cash register, which they learned to operate proficiently. And they replaced their ice-filled crates with real refrigerators, which kept their produce much fresher, much longer. They were so successful that they were ready to train several other men and women with similar backgrounds to duplicate their successful project in another part of town.

The Labor Department should have singled out this project as a model for the way federal training programs should work. But officials at Labor were obviously not impressed that Mr. Kendricks had helped this band of ex-criminals to become responsible, hard-working, productive citizens. The project was singled out for termination.

The Labor Department objected to Mr. Kendricks' decision to allow the trainees to make a profit from their work with the co-op. They refused to accept the fact that the profit motive was necessary to give the trainees incentive to get out of bed and go to the market at four o'clock in the morning, to refrain from stealing from the cash register, or to learn the essentials of running a business.

Because of their disregard for the fact that disadvantaged people, like all others, respond to incentives, the liberals have been utter failures at helping needy people improve their condition. No matter what their reason, the simple fact is that the liberals closed down a CETA project that was proving successful.

Fortunately, some of these CETA recipients took matters into their own hands. They started the same operation all over again or went into some other small enterprise. But others stayed on the street.

Conservatives need to point out that the liberals have no interest in making people independent and self-sufficient. Instead, they have a vested interest in keeping people dependent on their programs. The liberals have a vested interest in preventing the problems from being solved.

That may seem cynical, but the facts have to be faced. Liberal politicans get elected by promising programs to address human needs. Say you're poor, and the liberals offer welfare. Say you're hungry, and the liberals offer food stamps. Say you're unemployed, and the liberals offer CETA. Say your children are uneducated, and the liberals offer to bus them across town.

But if the liberals woke up one morning and discovered that poverty had been eliminated, that there were no more poor people, they would not rejoice; for much of their political base would have been eroded.

If the Reagan-inspired economic recovery wiped out unemployment, for example, the liberals would not be happy. There would be one less program for them to defend. They would no longer be able to entice jobless voters by promising to plow more money into so-called job training programs. So the last thing liberals ever want to do is to solve the problems they claim to care about.

On the other hand, conservatives have no vested interest in poor people remaining poor. They are not in the business of unloading the wagon, as Jack Kemp puts it, they are in the business of filling it up. Conservatives have a vested interest in everyone being able to participate in the economy, to make money, to become middle class, and to realize his own potential. That's where the conservatives' political support is.

Conservatives fail to win black support because they fail to expose liberal hypocrisy. Liberals are, for example, quick to recommend actions for others that are totally different from what they do themselves.

In 1981, I headed a committee of citizens in Washington, D.C., who presented a ballot initiative for educational tax credits. Under the plan, D.C. taxpayers who paid for a child to attend a private or parochial school or who contributed financially to support special projects in the public schools would be eligible to take a credit on their local income taxes. The tax credit would have made it easier for the less affluent families to exercise a choice in deciding which schools are best for their children.

Virtually everyone in the local political and education establishment opposed our committee. The chief spokesman for the opposition was the City Council Chairman, Arrington Dixon, whose two children happened to be enrolled in a private school.

Mr. Dixon argued that his children had special needs. We asked, in response, "Don't all children have special educational needs, Mr. City Council Chairman?"

Politicans and the education establishment were not alone in their hypocrisy. The news media also had their share of people who plotted one course for themselves and an entirely different course for others. On July 9, 1981, a column by Richard Cohen of *The Washington Post* attacked our initiative as "obnoxious." He characterized parents' efforts to seek alternatives from the D.C. public school system as follows: "[The initiative] goes to the heart of the notion of community: what we owe others. There is a notion . . . that the strong have an obligation to the weak, the educated for the uneducated, the rich for the poor. It is Christian. It is Jewish. It is Muslim. It is, for crying out loud, basic."

But as he set his unkind and unfair words to type, Cohen was compelled to admit that his child attended a private school. It could only be assumed that Cohen enrolled his daughter there because he had concluded that the private school would provide her with a better quality education than that offered by the public schools.

Why, then, did Cohen speak so negatively of an effort to

help other parents do the very same thing he had chosen to do? For him, selection of an alternative from the failing public schools was only proper. But for others to make the same choice, he argued, would be un-Christian, un-Jewish, un-Muslim, and un-basic.

Dorothy Gilliam, a liberal black columnist for *The Washington Post*, wrote in the October 12, 1981, edition of the paper:

> With my strong feelings about the importance of an education in mind, a decade or so ago we made the difficult choice to send our children to private schools. The revolution of black consciousness was in full swing but the D.C. public schools were in chaos. We just did not feel we could sacrifice our children's education during the school system's long climb forward. We debated whether to move to the suburbs where there was a better certainty that the youngsters would learn the three Rs well, or to stay in the city and send them to private schools. We chose to stay. We are lucky—few have the opportunity to make such a choice. Yet, deep within, I have always known that it will be the nation's public schools, not the private ones, that will be the salvation for the majority of black people.

In other words, the public schools were not adequate for her children, but they were fine for everyone else's children. She would not sacrifice her children's education, but she thought it was appropriate for other parents to sacrifice their children's education for the purpose of fulfilling the liberal social agenda.

Walter Mondale, George McGovern, and Jesse Jackson all enrolled their children at St. Albans, an exclusive private school in Washington, while telling everyone else to be "committed" to the public school system, whether the public schools are giving their children what they deserve or not.

Still another reason why conservatives fail to gain black support is that they have neglected to go wherever the liberals are and refute their misstatements of fact. The liberals' rationalizations for the persistence of critical social and economic problems in spite of massive federal expenditures should be answered with common-sense arguments that any thinking person can understand.

When asked about their plans for solving black youth unemployment, liberals have often begun their responses by bemoaning "the racism that permeates our society." Their implication is that the labor market is controlled by racists who have collectively decided to keep blacks out.

Conservatives should be there to say to the liberals, "You know, in the late 1940s and early 1950s, unemployment among black men was typically about the same as, and sometimes lower than, the rate for young white men. Today, unemployment is about three times more severe for black youth than for white youth. So are you trying to say that racism is three times worse today than it was in the 1940s and the 1950s?" After the liberals are forced to admit that their rationalizations make no sense, conservatives can pin them down on the fact that it is liberal policies that are the real culprit.

Many studies have proved beyond a shadow of a doubt that the minimum wage is like a sharp dagger in the backs of the black unemployed. By increasing the minimum wage several times over the last few decades, liberals have continued to make the dagger sharper and sharper. But since they have been successful at diverting everyone's attention from the real issues, few blacks recognize the harm liberals have done.

Another reason why conservatives fail to gain black support is that, when it comes to blacks, conservatives pay far too much attention to liberals who will never agree with them, and spend precious little time reinforcing blacks who have fought alongside them for conservative causes. Conservatives associated with the Reagan Administration have been particularly guilty of this deadly political sin.

During the 1980 campaign, so-called black leaders coalesced to support the reelection of President Jimmy Carter —not because they thought Carter was so great, but because they absolutely hated Ronald Reagan. These liberals were opposed to everything Reagan stood for.

These liberal blacks mounted a vigorous effort to portray Reagan as an enemy to blacks, an insensitive racist who somehow would roll back the clock on black economic progress and reverse gains made in the area of civil rights. The viciousness of their campaign was epitomized by a political cartoon that showed Reagan dressed in a Ku Klux Klan outfit. This cartoon, like many articles and columns accusing Reagan of being a racist, was clearly an outgrowth of the efforts of these black leaders to portray Reagan in the most unfavorable light possible.

Reagan, however, benefited from the efforts of such blacks as J. A. Parker, Thomas Sowell, Walter E. Williams, and E. V. Hill. Though they were obviously distressed over the shellacking Reagan took in the black community and were offended by their opponents' vicious campaign, the greatest distress and offense was dealt them by Reagan himself. During the transition period, Reagan ignored the conservatives and met with the Black Leadership Forum, a group comprised of heads of major black political organizations, principal instigators of the vicious attacks against him only thirty days before.

After the inauguration, Reagan turned that unfortunate mistake into a pattern. The first black person invited to a State Dinner at the White House was not one of his prominent conservative supporters, but Vernon Jordan, then president of the National Urban League.

The signal these occurrences sent to black Americans

was that, if one wanted to be heard or recognized by conservatives, the way to do it would be not by supporting them, but by fighting viciously against them. If conservatives are interested in expanding black participation in the conservative movement, this is not the signal to send.

A great deal depends upon the conservatives' success in bringing more blacks into their political movement. Forty years of liberal policy-making in Washington has been a disaster for black Americans.

Chapter Three

GOING ON THE MORAL OFFENSIVE

The prevailing conviction at the Third Generation discussions is that conservatives in the past behaved too defensively when making their case. Liberals made tremendous gains during the sixties by showing moral outrage and screaming "McCarthyism" whenever anyone criticized a liberal foreign policy position. Third Generation participants agree that it is high time for conservatives to demonstrate open disgust over the destructiveness and moral bankruptcy of liberal policy prescriptions in every area of American life. Conservatives have no reason to apologize for being on the side of individual liberty either at home or abroad.

RALPH REED: The setting is Athens, Georgia, home of the University of Georgia, where I was a wet-behind-the-ears freshman marginally active in Republican Party politics on campus. It is the first week of November 1979, and Jimmy Carter is (sad to report) President of the United States. Just days earlier, a group of radical Muslim students charged the U.S. Embassy in Tehran, seizing 52 Americans as hostages. The news of the hostage crisis, and Jimmy Carter's feeble response to events in Iran, leads every network newscast and headlines every newspaper in the nation.

On this particular evening in early November 1979, the films committee at the University of Georgia was showing *Patton,* starring George C. Scott. I happened to go to see that film on the night in question and was surprised to find the auditorium packed wall-to-wall for both the early and the late shows. Students streamed to the theater from every corner of the campus that night to see *Patton,* a film that celebrated U.S. greatness and military might. Hundreds were turned away when tickets sold out.

Toward the end of the film, when Patton is in trouble with the Allied High Command for his anti-Soviet remarks, there is a scene in which he receives a phone call from General Eisenhower. Although the audience hears only Patton's end of the conversation, Eisenhower's general remarks are clear: lay off the Soviets. Patton responds: "Ike, we are going to have to fight the Russians sooner or later. Why don't we get it over with now while we've got the tanks and the men over here already?"

Patton's remark at this point in the film elicited a spontaneous and uproarious standing ovation from the students in the audience. For several minutes, the theater was the scene of near pandemonium. Several hundred college students cheering a call to arms is something I shall not forget. I became convinced at that moment that a political earthquake was taking place within my generation, a shift in values and attitudes that would have major consequences for the future direction of the nation.

After the movie was over, more than one thousand students crossed paths, some leaving the early show, others coming to the late show. About a dozen students gathered in front of the student center to chant slogans against the Ayatollah in Iran. They hung an effigy of Khomeini from a nearby tree. Within a few minutes they had attracted a crowd of several hundred students chanting "First Strike Now!" The effigy shortly went up in flames, and the students headed down the main thoroughfare in Athens, where they paraded through the streets waving American flags and chanting pro-American slogans. The mob was finally broken up by police around midnight.

I can honestly say that I will remember that night for the rest of my life. Although I was a spectator rather than a participant in the events I have described, the spontaneous outpouring of patriotism and outrage at those (especially Jimmy Carter) who were failing to defend our nation corresponded exactly to my own feelings. I believe it was on that night, in the final year of the Carter Administration and in the midst of the Iranian hostage crisis, that I became a member of the "Third Generation" and embarked on the beginning of seven years of organizing conservative and Christian young people on our nation's campuses.

Generational consciousness is a consequence of shared experiences and grievances, not shared birth dates. What we call the "Third Generation" of conservatives cannot and should not be delineated by some arbitrary date of birth (i.e., anyone born between 1950 and 1970) but rather by certain specific and, in some cases, traumatic, shared experiences. We view ourselves as a generational unit because we share a common experience of political and social (and often, religious) consciousness. Generations, I believe, are not born; they are created.

Our shared experience is what has caused us to come together in forums and organizations that stress our generation's common interests. Most generational theorists have argued that generations are formed by a shared cataclysmic experience: war, famine, economic depression. In this sense, some have sought to explain European fascism by referring to the disillusionment and anger born in the trenches of World War I. David Halberstam, in his Pulitzer Prize-winning book, *The Best and the Brightest,* has argued that the Kennedy Administration's policies leading to the

Vietnam conflict can be explained by a paranoia about another Munich, a fear that Halberstam believes was shared by the entire generation that fought in World War II.

What is the defining, cataclysmic shared experience of the "Third Generation"? I believe it is a period of domestic upheaval and malaise that falls roughly within the years 1973 and 1980, when America experienced what might be termed a kind of domestic Seven Years War. From 1973 to 1980, we witnessed the Watergate scandal, the resignation in disgrace of Richard Nixon, the fall of Saigon, the hyperinflation of the late 1970s, the Carter Presidency, and the Iranian hostage crisis. During this domestic Seven Years War, the United States was not at war with any foreign foe, the Vietnam conflict having officially ended in 1973. Instead, the U.S., crippled by self-doubt and self-criticism, was at war within itself. This nation began to doubt whether it was the greatest country on earth, and even whether it was any better than the Soviet Union.

Watergate, Vietnam, the debacle of the Carter Presidency, and the election of Ronald Reagan comprise the shared experience that has led to the generational consciousness of this "Third Generation." Born in war and raised in scandal, we were told as teenagers that the best days for our nation were over; we were lectured by Jimmy Carter that America had to live within limits. We are a generation hungry to feel good about our country. Our generation is unique among all previous generations in U.S. history, in that we have witnessed both the first resignation of a U.S. President and the first defeat of U.S. soldiers on foreign soil. These were traumatic experiences, difficult to make sense of when experienced at a tender age, and I believe our generation shares a common grievance against those American leaders who made us feel downright guilty to be Americans. No wonder President Reagan enjoys his highest level of support among 18-to-30 year-olds: He is the first national leader in our lifetimes who has made us feel good about our country. We are a generation hungry for national and spiritual renewal.

LAURA INGRAHAM: I think the young conservatives of the eighties have borrowed much from the radicals of the sixties, and that accounts for why we have, perhaps, put a little fear into the hearts of liberals. Conservatism does not mean preserving the status quo or business as usual. Conservatism today means a restructuring of society on conservative principles. Government today at all levels consumes about 40 percent of the Gross National Product. We want to shift a great deal of the public sector spending into the private sector. We would like a top tax rate of about 10 percent. This is a pretty radical agenda.

We have even borrowed much of the language of the Left. College Republicans a few years ago had buttons and bumper stickers that said, "Smash the State." The anticommunist resistance movements operating inside Soviet-controlled territories are called National Liberation Movements. Conservatives today want social justice, which does not mean income redistribution, but that people are entitled to keep what they earn and to have equal protection under the law. Conservatives are taking away the platitudes and buzzwords of the Left.

I got my first experience as an activist at *The Dartmouth Review*. Like the editors of, say, *Ramparts* or the *Berkeley Barb* of the sixties campus Left, we enjoyed making fun of the establishment and caused something of a national uproar. Our paper, of course, had serious points to make, but we tried to make them with humor and satire. We wanted it to be fun to read. We wanted to create an atmosphere in which the establishment types would sit around all week nervously anticipating the next *Dartmouth Review* outrage and unable to predict from which direction the next attack would come.

We learned from the Left the value of good investigative reporting. We did not have a tradition of investigative journalism from a conservative perspective to imitate. Conservatives have generally not been attracted to journalism. So we imitated the Left—the Seymour Hershes, the Woodwards and Bernsteins. We learned that it could be fun to phone professors and college officials and merely quote them, to go into classrooms and report what was said and what was taught.

You see, many liberals on campus have grown so comfortable with their assumptions that they have forgotten how to answer conservative arguments. It is as if they stopped thinking 20 years ago—as if they are stuck in a time warp. Conservatives used to be like that, which is why they were on the intellectual and moral defensive back then. But we have learned from our mistakes and our complacency. And maybe we have changed some of our views over the past two decades.

We are not, for example, the tools of corporate America, as liberals seem to think. We are opposed to big bank bailouts, taxpayer-subsidized loans to General Motors, and farm subsidies. We think it is a national disgrace that Beverly Hills gets a community development block grant and that Hilton has used Urban Development Action Grants to build high-rise luxury hotels. And we do not believe that it is the responsiblity of middle America to guarantee the Chrysler Corporation against failure, so that Lee Iacocca can drive around in a limousine and write a book about what a brilliant entrepreneur he is. I, too, probably could make a profit and look brilliant if I were being financed by the government.

Conservatives are not defending the existing establishment, which has grown up as a result of essentially a half century of unbridled, unchecked liberalism. We are attempting to undo the vast web of special interest political payoffs that has developed over the years as well as the moral corruption that goes with it.

It is easy to make fun of liberal hypocrisy—to point out, for example, that the leader of the divestment from South Africa movement at Dartmouth drove a GM car, even while General Motors had extensive investments in South Africa. Liberals still haven't explained to my satisfaction why it is that blacks from neighboring countries, such as Mozambique, are desperately trying to get into South Africa. It makes good fodder for writers on campus conservative newspapers when black militants hang in effigy another black student who disagrees with their position on South Africa, which happened at Dartmouth recently. So much for the free speech movement that developed on the Berkeley campus in the sixties.

Conservatives also are becoming more sophisticated when it comes to the use of the media to get their views across. The 70 or so conservative college newspapers that have sprung up around the country in the wake of *The Dartmouth Review* are proving to be excellent training grounds for aspiring investigative journalists.

And since the Left is still well-entrenched in the academic establishment, there is tremendous opportunity for campus conservative activists to be confrontational. I have found, upon coming to Washington, that the liberal point of view is also comfortably entrenched in the government bureaucracy, for the obvious reason that the bureaucrats' personal and financial interests are tied up with the liberal social agenda. As a result, there is tremendous opportunity for adversarial conservative journalism in Washington. I have found the existing Washington establishment to be a larger version of Dartmouth's. I do not think the conservative movement has taken full advantage of this situation, in part, I suppose, because *The Washington Post* is the dominant newspaper in the city.

In the 1960s, the Left never allowed the enemy, that is, us, to frame the issues. But we still allow them to establish the parameters of the debate. We are still too passive. We accept their terms. We need to be more vigorous intellectually, more combative and morally indignant. We need to express moral outrage over what liberalism's policy prescriptions have done to people's lives at home and abroad.

In the United States, liberalism has created a permanent welfare class doomed to generations of poverty. Like heroin addicts, the poor have become dependent on handouts from the liberal politician. The result has been the devastation of the family. It has affected particularly the black family of the inner cities, the primary target of liberalism's programs, as government has taken over from the father the role of provider. This tragedy has been documented extensively by George Gilder, Charles Murray, Bill Moyers (in a television documentary), and others.

Liberalism's policy of appeasement has led to the slaughter and imprisonment of literally millions of people at the hands of communists. Liberals still cannot bring themselves to criticize communism seriously, despite the hellholes it creates wherever it takes hold.

We conservatives need to demonstrate our moral outrage. Liberals led us to these turns of events. We should not let them off the hook. They still have not let the Right off the hook for McCarthy's tactics in the fifties, which, in fact, had a negligible effect on the population. Yes, perhaps some were unjustly accused by Joseph McCarthy. But what of the millions who died at the hands of Pol Pot, in the Southeast Asian gulag, and in Afghanistan after the Soviet invasion? What of the Vietnamese boat people? What of President Carter's giving $132 million in U.S. assistance to the Sandinistas, thus helping Daniel Ortega to consolidate his grip over the Nicaraguan people and establish a Soviet military presence in the Americas? We have to hammer these themes home relentlessly. These were the results of liberal policies in the seventies, and liberals are pursuing the same policies today.

If liberalism's political mistake is to overplay its hand, conservatism errs in failing to go in for the kill. We do not do nearly enough in terms of using the moral and rhetorical weapons available. By hammering away on Joe McCarthy's sins, liberals have made it impossible for conservatives to point out that there are people in this country who are, in fact, working in concert with the enemy. In doing so, the liberals made it difficult for conservatives even to criticize liberal policies. In McCarthy they created an effective bogeyman.

We need a bogeyman of our own. Sydney Schanberg of *The New York Times* might be a good candidate. In Cambodia, he puffed up the Khmer Rouge and attacked the government allied with the United States. Perhaps more than anyone in the U.S. he contributed to the holocaust that ensued there. Through his distortions he provided the ammunition needed by the Left in the U.S. to relentlessly attack this country's policy in Southeast Asia. He succeeded in weakening America's will to defend a loyal ally under attack by a ruthless communist aggressor. Plenty of journalists in key positions on *The Washington Post* and *The New York Times* are guilty of, well, Schanbergism. We need to show them for what they are.

Liberalism, today, is on the intellectual and moral defensive. It is time for conservatives to finish off liberalism culturally. We need to expose their movies, books, magazines. We need to organize protests and picket marches against Chevron for propping up the Soviet and Cuban-installed regime in Angola through its oil operation. We need to make it uncomfortable to be a liberal in the 1980s, just as the liberals made it unpleasant to be a conservative in the 1960s and 1970s. We have to demonstrate vocally and visibly that it's morally and intellectually untenable to be a liberal anymore.

PETER FERRARA: In my view, the Third Generation's formative development has been strongly influenced by certain compelling and decisive experiences of recent history. We have seen the massive economic failure of socialism, not to mention communism, as compared to democratic, free market, entrepreneurial capitalism. Within our generation, except for a tiny band of fools, the idealistic appeal of socialism and communism is entirely dead. Big government is routinely recognized as a counterproductive joke. The excitement and idealism today is over how to create new economic opportunity and prosperity through free markets and more economic freedom.

In addition, it is impossible to seriously maintain that the Soviet Union has a desirable government under which to live or that we should emulate it—a notion that had some credence in certain circles in the 1930s, 1960s, and 1970s. Afghanistan, Poland, Cambodia, the treatment of Soviet dissidents, the shooting down of passenger flight KAL-007, the murder of Major Arthur Nicholson in East Germany, the plot to assassinate the Pope, and other events have thoroughly convinced young people of the evil and brutality of the Soviets and their proxies.

The most important factor in politics over the long run is idealism. It motivates people to get involved and to commit their time, energy, and resources. It creates political excitement and momentum. Today, conservatives have become idealists, advancing economic freedom, opportunity, and prosperity along with traditional values at home and encouraging the fight against totalitarian slavery abroad.

The renewed commitment to idealism by the conservative movement's major political leaders is the key source of growing conservative power today.

This renewed idealistic commitment has led to the outpouring of new ideas and proposals that have put conservatives on the moral and political offensive. Such proposals, well-articulated, are what dominate politics and set the national agenda.

The social issues have been a big plus for conservative Republicans. This is because the people most concerned about these issues are traditional Democratic voters—Southerners, blue-collar workers, ethnics. For a conservative Republican, these issues can be on the cutting edge of politics, bringing new and traditionally Democratic voters into the Republican fold.

Reducing the welfare state through tax cuts has been another potent political weapon deployed by conservatives in their war against government spending. Focusing first on tax cuts has allowed conservatives to take a popular, positive initiative.

The greatest political challenge facing the Third Generation is how to reform the welfare state, transforming U.S. society back into an opportunity society, sharply reducing government spending and the claim it represents on the economic lives of free men and women, while still addressing the desirable goals of welfare state programs.

This can be done by focusing primarily on basic structural reforms of government, seeking to achieve desirable goals through means involving much less government spending, either through greater reliance on the private sector, or through revamped, rational government programs. Privatization, welfare reform, and the New Federalism are all ideas that will allow us to reduce government spending dramatically and at the same time perform even better the functions that the public demands.

In regard to regulation, we should advocate free trade, foreign and domestic. Any regulatory restriction that prevents two adults from trading with each other on terms upon which they mutually agree should be attacked on both moral and economic grounds. We should work to repeal all protectionist measures as a pro-consumer cause.

On the social issues, we must recognize that the social conservatives are key, powerful, central, and indispensable players in the conservative movement. They are bringing millions of new voters and activists into the conservative camp, individuals who can easily come to embrace the entire conservative agenda. The political challenge we face is how to maintain faith with the social conservatives without scaring away the so-called yuppies. This can be accomplished by upholding traditional values in a nonthreatening way. To do this, we should emphasize, as our central policy goal in this area, freedom for those who hold traditional beliefs to practice them without imposing them on others. The only issue that does not fit into this theme is abortion, which involves a conflict between two human lives. Here we cannot shy away from opposition to abortion. And, politically, there is no reason why we must.

I see no political problem with saying that the Soviet communists and their system are evil and dangerous. Voters ultimately always choose a foreign policy of strength and vigor rather than weakness and appeasement. This has been borne out in election after election, even at the height of the Vietnam War. In this light, we must support freedom fighters for the purpose of rolling back the Soviets. Whenever American troops are used, the goal must be for them to win and get out. This requires overwhelming the enemy with power and force. We must never again send U.S. soldiers into battle under no-win restraints, as in Vietnam or in Lebanon.

Chapter Four

FAITH AND POLITICS

Millions of new voters, including registered Democrats and those previously uninterested in politics, are streaming into the conservative fold. They are concerned about what their children are taught in school; about the perverted material in such TV shows as **Three's Company** *or Larry Flynt's* **Hustler** *magazine that bombard their households every day; and about the increasingly "value-free" quality of American society. They are angry that voluntary prayer is illegal in public schools while Marxist study groups are perfectly acceptable, even desirable. Most of all, they are horrified by the legalized slaughter of millions of human lives in abortion clinics, many financed by the taxpayer.*

ROY JONES: What I have to say this evening, and I will be quite frank with you, comes from the heart. There is something that disturbs me about the conservative movement. It is that conservative organizations, especially conservative youth organizations as a group, have been very shy about dealing with the moral and social justice issues.

Such issues are of deep concern to me and of deep concern to many young people across this country. Many of them, who are attending predominantly religious schools, have no real interest in economic policy, foreign affairs, or national defense. The issues that hit them in the gut, that have convinced them to get involved in the political process, are voluntary school prayer and the right to life.

I would like to focus, first, on why this group of young people is mainly interested in social issues; and, second, on how we might be able to expand their interest to include the entire range of conservative issues so that they might begin to see the relationship between moral issues and economic and national security policy.

We are talking about a very large number of students and young people. In the Protestant community alone, there are more than 25,000 religious elementary and secondary schools with nearly three million students enrolled. As a matter of fact, three such schools are formed every day in this country. Most of these young people come from Protestant backgrounds that are conservative and even fundamentalist. A lot of conservatives either have not known or have refused to accept this reality. No one issue has affected young people in this country today more than abortion. There are those who contend that persons who become involved in the political process because of a deep-seated religious belief ought to be excluded from the political debate. When religiously motivated people are involved in politics, they are often portrayed by the elitist press, television networks, and liberal politicians as being in violation of the separation of church and state.

Such critics, however, do not know history. Religious belief played an enormous role in the founding of this country. America's heritage is based upon the presupposition of the existence of God, as well as the idea that His servants, you and I, ought to be involved in the democratic process. The first settlers who came to this country did so because they wanted religious freedom. They wanted to go to a land where they could freely practice their religious beliefs without fear of persecution and discrimination.

The founders of America wholeheartedly believed that in order to have democracy there needed to be religious freedom. That is what this country is based upon. Scripture says, "Where the Spirit of the Lord is, there is liberty." That is what I believe, and that is what nearly three million religious elementary and secondary school kids across this country believe.

School prayer should not be segregated from the issue of free speech. School prayer is a First Amendment issue. It is a civil rights issue. There is a mass exodus from the public schools today. One of the reasons, I believe, is that students are fleeing state-sanctioned religious persecution and discrimination. Do these people have a right to get involved in the political process? I think they do.

There are a lot of religious students who have to stick it out in public schools because they cannot afford private schools or because there are no inexpensive religious schools in their area, though there probably would be if there were education vouchers. These students are forced to confront administrators every day who tell them it is against the law for them to practice their religious faith on school property. These students are told they have to shove their God and faith in a locker until after the last school period.

Students, like those in Catonsville, Maryland, have to hide in hallways every day to hold a prayer meeting. At the end of their prayer session, they have to change the location of their next meeting to another hallway, in another area of the building, so that they are not caught the following day and punished by school officials. Olivia Mendez, an eight-year-old second grader from Sanford, Florida, was disciplined and publicly humiliated in front of schoolmates at a Christmas party for passing out Christmas cards with the word "Jesus" on them. I have more than a thousand such cases that are documented and sitting in my office right now. Luckily, Olivia has strong parents, who are challenging this in court with the help of Concerned Women of America. Despite the fact that she was humiliated by her teacher in front of her classmates, Olivia went back to school this September. These are the kinds of heroes, in my view, that can turn America around.

I have found in my dealings with young people who are motivated by their religious convictions that they not only have become political but are oriented toward becoming activists. These young people have grown used to confrontation. They have little respect for state authorities who routinely attempt to destroy their religious faith. They want to change the system.

I have been personally involved in the formation of a new group called the Conservative Youth Federation. One of our major goals is to reach out to these religious schools. I believe the time has finally come, thanks to the heightened political involvement of the religious community, for conservative leaders, young and old, to begin reaching out to religious students all over this country. If we begin to incorporate religious youth into the conservative movement, swelling our numbers and, just as important, taking advantage of their inherent activism, we will change the entire political equation and the context in which we debate these issues.

Even if a small percentage of the three million Protestant students in religious schools today get actively involved in conservative politics, we will shake up the liberal establishment still embedded in Washington. We have to develop a means of telling these students that they can make a difference by joining the conservative movement. We need to involve them in conservative organizations and expose them to other important issues, issues they might know nothing about.

No one is telling them about Central America or about the communist threat to their way of life. No one is telling them about how the federal government, through a progressive income tax, has undermined the family unit and the ability of Americans to become self-reliant. Our responsiblity is to tell them about free enterprise and about the misery and poverty caused by Marxism, socialism, and all forms of economic redistribution.

The religious youth of this country are a tremendous untapped resource for conservatives. They are waiting to be organized.

DAVID MASON: About two months ago, Ben Hart circulated a questionnaire to the Third Generation group, asking them to rate the importance of various issues in domestic policy, national security, and social concerns. The vast majority of the group rated the social issues, in particular prayer in school and abortion, dead last, with economic and defense policy finishing well in front.

These results were, quite frankly, rather shocking to me, because my idea of what conservatism stands for is quite different from the opinions expressed in Ben Hart's survey. It is my opinion that the moral and social issues are vitally important in at least two respects.

One is that the moral issues, like school prayer, like abortion, are extremely important in attracting a constituency that will form a conservative majority. The second is that a moral outlook on the part of candidates and the Republican Party is a crucial element in allowing conservatives to take the moral offensive. Liberals have used this tactic very successfully to beat conservatives over the head. Well, now we have our moral issues. *Roe v. Wade* was clearly a constitutionally unsound decision, and abolishing prayer from the public schools is clearly a violation of First Amendment rights.

I have found in my experience with grass-roots conservative activists, activists outside the D.C. beltway, that their concerns are somewhat different from the opinions reflected in the Third Generation survey. The Third Generation in Washington is made up mainly of sophisticated political pros. Sophisticated, inside-the-beltway types are, in general, slightly embarrassed about the social issues. They seem somewhat messy in urbane company. It is not easy to talk about closing down abortion clinics or about allowing kids to pray.

There is a gut-wrenching, emotional component to these issues that makes it much easier for Washington-based conservatives to focus on economic issues, funding the contras, the Strategic Defense Initiative, and the Soviet threat. Conservatives feel comfortable talking with liberals about economics and national security. The liberals won't sneer and turn their backs on conservatives if such subjects are raised. But talk about Jerry Falwell, Phyllis Schlafly, or Pat Robertson, and many inside-the-beltway conservatives will say, "Well, I don't agree with Falwell personally, but we need him to register votes. We need him to build the conservative coalition." They will take a condescending attitude toward people interested in the social issues. The political professionals should know that social conservatives feel the condescension and are getting tired of it. They are fed up with constantly being told: "We'll get to your issues later, when we've won our other battles."

The fact is, many grass-roots conservatives, especially in the South, care more about abortion and prayer in school than about tax cuts. They think economic policy is important, but their strongest feelings are evoked by the social issues. In every campaign I have been a part of, it has been the social conservatives who have worked the hardest stuffing envelopes, registering voters, and going door to door. You cannot win elections without them. It is as simple as that.

To borrow an analysis from Morton Blackwell, the traditional Republican coalition of businessmen and people who are concerned about the Soviet threat and international communism makes up about 40 to 45 percent of the electorate. If you run on a platform of cutting spending, taxes, and government red tape and fighting communism, you will get a solid 40 to 45 percent of the vote. The other side, in other words, will win a landslide election every time if those are your only issues.

Social issues are the ones that garner the other 10 to 15 percent that conservatives need for victory. And it is the social issues that hit in the gut. We had 30,000 pro-lifers marching in Washington on the anniversary of *Roe v. Wade.* You could not find 30,000 people to march for a tax cut, or deregulation, or SDI, or budget cuts. As important as these issues are, they do not move people to go out in the streets. Though I oppose it, abortion clinics have been bombed. How many people have tried bombing the IRS, Legal Services, the Interstate Commerce Commission, the Labor Department? No one that I know of.

It is true that the economic and national security conservatives constitute the majority of our coalition in terms of numbers. But they are not motivated as much as the social conservatives, who believe that what is happening in those abortion clinics is essentially a replay of the Holocaust. They think people are being killed, legally, in a federally funded, constitutionally protected facility, and they feel there is something fundamentally immoral about U.S. government policy. This feeling is on a different plane, a different level, than simply the opinion that the government is too burdensome, or that the economic policies being followed slow down commerce. This is why it is the social conservatives who are out there ringing doorbells. The communist threat is a long way off—overseas somewhere. But it is in the local schools that kids are told it is illegal for them to pray. It is right in town here that there is a constitutionally protected abortion facility, where literally hundreds of babies are killed every week.

Moreover, I believe that there is a yearning for morality, at least I'd like to call it that, in the body politic. One of the insurance companies in Hartford, Connecticut, does a regular poll on attitudes of the American people. About three years ago, they dropped a number of religious questions into the poll. The results confirmed the importance of religion to the American people in so overwhelming a manner that the first reaction of the pollsters was to disbelieve it. They did the poll again and came up with exactly the same results. So have the Reagan polls, which is one reason Reagan comes out so strongly in favor of religious values whenever he speaks to any gathering of religious leaders.

All you have to do is look at the growth in recent years of the evangelical churches to know this is the case. How many of these churches are springing up every year is nothing short of phenomenal. I think we are seeing a true religious revival in the U.S., and with it, a serious change in the political equation of what it takes to get elected.

Why has this happened? I think it is because the values that the U.S. has stood for over the course of 200 years have been eroded, almost beyond recognition, by the Democratic Party's liberal welfare state. The ideas of self-reliance, that America is a place worth defending, worth laying down one's life for, that God counts, have been under consistent attack by liberals for many decades now as well as by many of the elites running the big establishment institutions, such as the media, government, and the major universities. People are reacting against this steady erosion of basic American values.

Jeane Kirkpatrick wrote an article some time ago on why conservative Democrats do not become Republicans. The answer, she said, is that Republicans are interested only in providing the necessities—a good economy, a strong defense, and so on—but are reluctant to take on the moral leadership of the country. To ask people to sacrifice for the defense of a nation, we first have to convince people that there is something here beyond self-interest worth defending, some higher moral purpose that makes it important for the country to continue to exist. It seems to me that libertarianism fails to do this. It is not a philosophy that can unite the country, that people can rally around. It is not viable politically. People, in general, want more from their leaders. For evidence, just look at the great leaders throughout history. Their message was always one of moral urgency: Churchill, Lincoln, Washington, and yes, I would say Reagan—hardly Cato Institute-style libertarians. They were all great leaders because people believed their message was important and, in the case of the first three, worth dying for.

We do not want people to get the idea that the U.S. is just an alternative political arrangement that justifies itself according to the latest GNP statistics. Libertarianism cannot work politically because it fails to recognize the fundamental nature of man as a moral and religious being. Religion is one of man's strongest impulses, so it behooves politicians to take this fact into account.

There is an important philosophical point here. If God and ultimate salvation are not man's natural end, then the perpetuation of state power will become his overarching reason for living. Communists know this. They know that to build the strongest allegiance possible to the state on the part of the people, they must first destroy religion. Religious institutions—and I am speaking here mainly of the Judeo-Christian tradition—divert people's allegiance from the state. The communists know this, and thus they destroy religious institutions.

There is a strong parallel here between the elimination of religious institutions in communist countries and the hostility displayed toward religion by liberals. An anti-religious attitude is essential to collectivist philosophy. The more socialism there is, the more power is concentrated in the hands of the state, the more hostility to religion there is on the part of those in power.

Do not misunderstand me, I believe in the separation of church and state. I am merely pointing out that, to succeed in politics, it is important for politicians to present themselves as leaders who believe in fundamental moral and religious truths, principles that most people hold most dear and that most people think essential to the perpetuation of a good and free society. Obviously, the state has no business enforcing these principles. But it is a moral obligation, I believe, and I think most people believe, for our political leaders to be good role models for the rest of the country. It is important for voters to know that political power is not the politician's only goal in life and that he knows there is something far more important and profound worth living for.

I mentioned the incredible proliferation of new evangelical Christian churches. It is worth noting, I think, that the leaders and congregations of these churches are primarily young people in their twenties and thirties, people starting families. That is a fact worthy of attention by any aspiring politician in today's political climate. The desire for moral leadership may be strongest among our youngest voters.

RALPH REED: I believe there is a Christian revival going on, and that this is changing the U.S. political landscape. Revival has always been closely associated with national renewal in our history. The first Great Awakening in the eighteenth century helped lay the foundations for U.S. independence from Great Britain. The second Great Awakening in the 1840s and 1850s fueled the fires of abolitionism and created a cultural climate in which slavery could not survive. Similarly, the great outpouring of religious interest and enthusiasm in the 1980s threatens the survival of abortion on demand and the entire feminist-humanist agenda behind abortion. Historically, when Americans have hungered to feel good about their nation, they have almost always turned to God, and sweeping revivals have been the natural result. And although religious revivalism in the U.S. is primarily a spiritual phenomenon, it always has earth-shaking political consequences. It should be recalled that Republican, abolitionist candidates scored their biggest gains in the 1850s in upstate New York, the so-called burned-over districts where Charles Graddison Finney led the greatest revivals of the nineteenth century. There is more than a grain of truth to Jerry Falwell's remark that his purpose is to "get people saved, get them baptized, and get them registered to vote."

In the Third Generation, there has been an unprecedented interest in having a personal relationship with God. Although the Second Generation of conservatives, the founders of the New Right in the 1970s, pioneered the politicization of the Christian community, I believe the Third Generation is unique in its hunger for a very personal and intimate relationship with God. And as I have already suggested, I think this spiritual hunger is directly related to our desire to feel good about ourselves and our nation after the malaise of the 1970s. If the Second Generation registered Christians to vote, the Third Generation will go one step further: We will give Christians the opportunity to govern America, to take a leadership role in society as candidates, campaign managers, and Hill staffers.

Finally, and most important, I believe the Christians of

the Third Generation will be wiser and more prudent than their predecessors in the acquisition and use of political power. You can expect to see fewer Christian candidates running campaigns directly out of the churches, and more polished, capable candidates who also happen to be Christians. The Second Generation, I believe, has erred in generating within the Christian community what can only be called "zeal without knowledge." We have seen Christian candidates accuse their opponents of not being Christians, of being tools of Satan, while associating their own campaigns with the sanction of Almighty God. This is not as wrong as it is foolish. Americans historically are a very religious people, but they are also a very tolerant people, and they are frightened away from any person or party that associates its opponents with the Devil. Some of the truly tragic defeats of fine conservative, Christian candidates in the 1986 elections are strong evidence of the need for more wisdom and savvy by Christians in politics. We need more Christians who are interested in, and capable of, governing.

This is where I hope Students for America and similar groups can play a vital role in our nation's renewal. Students for America is a self-consciously generational vehicle. Its mission is to train and educate a generation of moral leadership. Students for America, I might emphasize, is not a Christian organization and does not require any spiritual litmus test for membership. By teaching young Christians to lead people who may or may not share their religious beliefs, we aim to teach them how to govern people who disagree with them on spiritual issues when they become candidates and officeholders later in life.

This, I trust, will be the legacy of not only Students for America, but the Third Generation as well: a generation that loves God with all its heart and that possesses the wisdom and understanding to put that love into effect in politics without scaring others away. My dear friend Morton Blackwell often says that we owe it to our principles to be effective. I think Christians in the Third Generation are learning that they owe it to their God not simply to be involved in politics but to be effective in politics. At the deepest and most profound levels of American politics, the revival of religion within the Third Generation is changing America by producing young people who love God above everything else in their lives, and who also possess the ability to govern this nation into the twenty-first century.

Chapter Five

CHURCH, SCHOOL, FAMILY, AND STATE

Of the subjects addressed at Third Generation forums, those issues relating to religion, the outlawing of prayer from public schools, First Amendment interpretation, special affirmative action privileges for homosexuals, and the state role in preventing the further moral decay of society stirred the most passion, sometimes leading to sharp philosophical divisions among the participants. The following are some representative remarks made during the discussions.

PRAYER IN SCHOOL

ADAM MEYERSON: As a Jew, I would prefer not to have prayer in public schools. I fear that prayers will be mostly Christian and that my children will feel excluded from their classmates. Prayers need not be a serious problem, however, if they are genuinely voluntary and if an atmosphere of tolerance and accommodation exists between religious majorities and minorities. So long as Jews and other religious minorities are treated courteously, sitting through

Christmas or Easter ceremonies need not be a terrible ordeal. In these days of rampant crime and drugs, worse things can happen to you in school. . . .

PATRICK MCGUIGAN: Prayer in public schools is a political issue in modern American politics because the Supreme Court exercised non-Constitutional powers when it removed the option for local communities and states to allow time for prayer or reflection at the start of the school day. The court was wrong to go as far as it did in its anti-prayer decisions. There should be protections for minorities who do not wish to participate. But the present state of affairs prevents the majority of school children and their parents from exercising their rights of religious freedom, which are specifically guaranteed in our founding document.

Prayer is only a political issue because the Court made it so. Those of us who believe in God either have to accept judicial rulings that are wrong or work aggressively to overturn those bad decisions and, further, change the composition of the Supreme Court.

PETER FERRARA: Prayer in public schools is a political issue because the schools are public, and consequently anything that happens there is a political issue. This whole problem would not exist if we had more access to a private education system.

In any event, even in public schools, students should be allowed to pray, silently or in unison, individually or in groups, in any circumstance in which they are otherwise allowed to express themselves voluntarily, including at all times during breaks, lunches, or other free time. This is simply civil libertarian doctrine applied consistently.

PORNOGRAPHY

PETER FERRARA: Citizens should organize boycotts against pornography. The government should not subsidize pornography. Seven-Eleven stores have pulled some of the men's magazines off their shelves, as have People's, Rite-Aid, Southland, Revco, and Dart drugstores. Thus we see that citizen boycotts work. For practical and political reasons, this should be the focus of conservative efforts against pornography, not campaigning to make it illegal.

GROVER NORQUIST: It seems that, when government gets involved in an issue like pornography, far less headway is made than when private citizens band together and boycott the businesses that sell it. Look at the ridicule the Meese commission on pornography has been subjected to. The Justice Department's decision to pursue this issue has actually slowed progress in the war against pornography. Americans get nervous when the Justice Department, or any government agency, begins closing down publications, no matter how distasteful. The government has failed in its war on poverty; it fails to deliver the mail on time; it cannot provide decent train service; it has failed to provide for our retirement; it cannot give adequate medical care; it is ineffectual in putting violent criminals in jail —why should we trust it with a campaign against pornography?

LEIGH ANN METZGER: Pornography. Right now it's about a $10 billion a year industry, most of which is under the control of organized crime. But before we can decide what to do about it, we ought to define it. Justice Potter Stewart once said, "I know it when I see it." *Webster's Dictionary* defines pornography as "writing about prostitutes. . . . writings, pictures, etc., intended primarily to arouse sexual desire." This definition was accepted by the 1978 Williams Commission in Great Britain and by the 1985–1986 U.S. Attorney General's Commission on Pornography.

The problem with such a definition is that it is extremely broad and does not even come close to drawing distinctions between the two extremes, which are currently characterized under the banner of "pornography." There is a vast difference between *Playboy* and *Hustler,* and still more between *Hustler* and "kiddie porn." At the farthest end of the spectrum are films in which people are dismembered, and the so-called snuff films, in which people are actually killed during a sexual act.

It is hard for me to imagine even the most ardent civil libertarian not wanting laws against some kinds of pornography. The debate is over what kinds of regulation and over what kinds of material. As you can see, the definition given in *Webster's* does not go very far. There is a universe of pornography that can be considered "sexually explicit material with an intent to arouse."

But under that umbrella there are several distinct categories: 1) obscenity, 2) indecency, and 3) other sexually explicit material that does not meet the legal definition of the first two. These separate categories require different kinds of regulation and action and enjoy different protections.

Obscenity is defined by the courts as "offensive to accepted standards of decency." In *Roth v. United States* (1957), the court stated that obscenity was not protected under the First Amendment. This definition, however, was updated in 1973 in *Miller v. California,* requiring a more strict definition of proof against the alleged pornographer.

The Miller test, as it is called, requires that one of the following conditions be met before a work can legally be classified as pornography:

1) The average person, applying contemporary community standards, finds that the work, taken as a whole, appeals to the prurient (lustful) interest.
2) The work depicts or describes in a patently offensive way sexual conduct specifically defined by the applicable state or federal law.
3) The work, taken as a whole, lacks serious literary, artistic, scientific, or political value.

Civil libertarians have charged that this last requirement is a kind of catch-all provision that allows the court wide discretion on the censorship of material it finds offensive. But this has not proved to be the case. In 1974, for example, the *Jenkins v. Georgia* ruling determined that the movie *Carnal Knowledge* was obscene on the grounds that it lacked any "serious literary, artistic, political, or scientific value." But the Supreme Court overturned the *Jenkins* ruling. And there have been no successful attempts to censor any such material since that decision. Thus, it hardly seems to be the case that the Miller test for pornography endangers our First Amendment protection.

Of the three groups I mentioned, obscenity requires the most rigid regulations. Obscenity is illegal under current law and carries the penalties of a federal criminal offense. However, it is perfectly legal for family grocery stores to sell a publication like *Hustler*. I would think that anyone who has seen that magazine would call it obscene. But it is not legally defined as such, proving that the current restriction on obscene material is hardly a threat to anyone's ability to express himself.

Indecency is applicable only to electronic communication. It falls under the jurisdiction of the FCC (Federal Communications Commission). The 1934 Communications Act provides that no obscene or indecent communications can be made over the broadcast media. This was affirmed in the 1978 *FCC v. Pacifica* case in which the Supreme Court ruled that the broadcast media are unique because anyone at any time can have access to the airwaves. Because the airwaves belong to everyone, some controls are required. This seems to me only common sense. A parent can't watch over a child every minute of the day to make sure he isn't switching on the "porn" channel.

The third category is other sexually explicit materials that do not meet the legal definition of obscenity or the FCC's definition of indecency. The types of material in this category are the so-called adult men's magazines, *Hustler, Penthouse,* and the like. This is constitutionally protected material.

But just as it is a First Amendment right to publish such stuff, at least as interpreted under current law, it is within our constitutional rights to oppose it. Many anti-pornography groups have been created to help citizens deal with pornography at the local level. Seven-Eleven stores have recently pulled the men's magazines off their shelves, at a cost of some $30 million a year to the porn industry. Seven-Eleven evidently realized that it was in its own financial interest to accede to the prevailing opinion in the communities in which their stores must do business, rather than to come down on the side of *Hustler's* Larry Flynt. The market can be a tremendous ally in the fight against pornography—either as individual protest, in person or by letter; or group protest, by picketing or boycotts. Such actions can produce enormous gains by hitting the porn business where it hurts—in the wallet.

Some so-called libertarians claim that citizen action is a violation of the pornographer's First Amendment rights.

This is ridiculous. Society often uses the marketplace to express what it wants. Moreover, the First Amendment belongs to all Americans, not just to pornographers. Community standards are determined locally by the citizens. If a community chooses to stand together, it can make it economic suicide for a business to promote smut, and people are fully within their rights to do so.

A concentrated effort against organized crime—putting, say, the top ten crime bosses behind bars—would go a long way toward eliminating porn. About 90 percent of the pornography produced is controlled by just a few people in organized crime. But the federal government also must enforce existing laws against obscene material. The FCC must enforce regulations against indecent material appearing in the broadcast media; communities should support those businesses that recognize and respect the values of the local citizens; politicians should stand strong as representatives of the people; and, finally, families should fulfill their duties as guardians of their children.

Pornography is a serious social illness. It reinforces the basest human instincts; it victimizes women; it funds organized crime; it has been linked to some of the vilest murders and acts of perversion known to man. Pornography has nothing to do with love and affection. It is a social disease that can be cured only through concentrated action on the part of the people.

ABORTION

ADAM MEYERSON: One of the most important purposes of goverment is to protect innocent human life. But the law should also be sensitive to the distress that unwanted pregnancy can cause in mothers. If this distress is genuinely severe, as for example after rape or incest, or if the mother's life is endangered, then abortion ought to be allowed. In all other cases of unwanted pregnancy, the mother should be able to count on the emotional support of her community as she bears her child . . . .

PATRICK MCGUIGAN: Abortion is wrong and should be forbidden. Short of this, the states should be empowered to deal with the abortion issue so they at least could limit the number of abortions. It is important to recall that no state had an abortion statute as "liberal" as the monstrosity the Supreme Court foisted on us in 1973.

Admittedly, the hard cases of rape are troubling and require a heartfelt and compassionate response. But the value of innocent human life is not lessened because it is the product of rape or incest, just as an unwanted pregnancy late in a woman's productive years results in a valuable innocent life.

A commitment to life requires us to provide meaningful alternatives to the horror of abortion. Each one of us dedicated to the right to life should do everything we can to provide support for unwed mothers. To support life is difficult, but I cannot think of any issue on which my feelings are stronger.

PETER FERRARA: Abortion is always wrong except when the life of the mother is threatened. Since pregnancy from rape or incest is rare, the question of abortion in these cases should not stand in the way of legislation prohibiting abortion in all other circumstances, which should be enacted and allowed by the Constitution.

Abortion does not involve the issue of whether a woman should be permitted to control her own body. It involves the issue of when a human being should be allowed to take the life of another. The political corner has been turned on this issue. The states will soon again be allowed to decide on their own abortion laws, with most prohibiting routine abortions.

GAY RIGHTS

ADAM MEYERSON: Castro's Cuba sends homosexuals to prison. So did Nazi Germany. That kind of persecution has no place in a free society. It is not the business of the state to police what consenting adults do in the privacy of their bedrooms. But private behavior is one thing. A public sanction for special "gay rights" is quite another. Private employers and landlords should not be forced to hire or rent to homosexuals if they do not want to. Homosexuals should not be put in the same category as blacks and women in anti-discrimination legislation. I also believe that homosexual bathhouses are a public health hazard and should be shut down.

PETER FERRARA: The government should not attempt to make homosexuality illegal. But those who do not wish to associate with homosexuals must be free not to do so, whether in employment, housing, restaurants, stores, or any other privately owned place. The situation is different than in the case of discrimination based on race, gender, religion, or ethnic origin, because there is no morally acceptable basis for discrimination on these grounds, but people should be free to refuse to associate with homosexuals.

For the same reasons, parents must be free to prevent homosexuals from teaching their children in schools. But homosexuals are deemed to have the same right to employment in a public institution as anyone else, which becomes another reason why education can no longer be provided adequately by the public sector.

PATRICK MCGUIGAN: Even if it is true that many homosexuals are "born that way," as they claim, their sexual conduct is a threat to a stable and moral society. I do not think the state or anyone else should seek to identify and vilify homosexuals. But at the same time I do not believe that we should accord them special legal status—such as giving them affirmative action privileges. Homosexuals as individuals deserve the same legal protections as any of us. But homosexuality as an act must remain outside the accepted realm of what some euphemistically label "sexual expression."

The Supreme Court—which today seems always to be looking for ways to undermine the moral fabric of society —recently allowed a lower court decision to stand which, in essence, says to the state of Oklahoma that it must allow practicing, public advocates of homosexuality to become school teachers and to remain school teachers—at a time when we are all increasingly concerned about the sexual abuse of children. Parents should have the right to prevent homosexuals who are aggressive advocates of sexual deviancy from teaching in the public schools.

SHOULD GOVERNMENT PROMOTE THE MORAL WELL-BEING OF AMERICA?

PATRICK MCGUIGAN: Some would argue that the government should remain neutral on moral questions. I would agree that such neutrality would be eminently preferable to the present state of affairs, in which government (particularly at the federal level) has become an active promoter of immorality. Government, ideally the protector of the innocent, has become the active partner in murder, as in the thoroughly despicable "Baby Doe" and other infanticide incidents. Government funds are used to pay for sex education materials that encourage support for so-called alternative lifestyles. There is a case to be made for government neutrality on moral issues, but there is no defense for government promoting immorality.

I am comfortable with the idea that government should promote the moral well-being of the people in the general sense. That is why I believe government should be as accommodating as possible toward religious organizations, showing sensitivity to the Sabbaths of the various denominations, allowing voluntary prayer in schools, allowing religious organizations to use public facilities in a regulated manner, and so forth.

PETER FERRARA: The government should end all activities that discourage the moral well-being of Americans or subsidize immmorality. Examples are government funding of abortions and the teaching of immoral behavior, i.e., the promotion of so-called alternative lifestyles, in the public schools. The government also should ensure that those who believe in traditional moral values are free to live in accordance with those beliefs without government restriction.

SHOULD DIVORCE BE ILLEGAL?

PATRICK MCGUIGAN: Much of the increase in marriage failure, I think, can be traced to the general decline in personal responsibility and accountability for one's actions. The divorce rate is a function of societal norms as reflected in the mainstream media, and by media I mean not only television and newspapers, but also music, radio, popular magazines, and books. As a society, we will help the stability of most marriages when there is a greater collective disdain for casual sex and disposable relationships.

I believe that it ought to be more difficult to get a divorce. But government's role here is peripheral to the central problem, which is the general, all too facile acceptance of promiscuity and its progeny. It was a real revelation to me, after four years in graduate school, when a female colleague thanked me because I had treated her as a friend and not as a potential sex partner. This seems to me to be a negative comment on the state of U.S. society and popular culture. It seems to me that it is the liberals, the very ones who complain most about sexual harassment, who are themselves guilty of a "mild" form of sexual harassment by promoting promiscuity and immoral behavior. Many feminists, in fact, have come to realize this. It is a point upon which they agree with many traditionalist conservatives.

IS AMERICA A CHRISTIAN COUNTRY?

PATRICK MCGUIGAN: The U.S. is a country founded upon the Judeo-Christian tradition. As Justice William Douglas once put it: "Americans are a religious people whose institutions presuppose a Supreme Being." Though the majority religion in this country is Christian, we must shy away from explicitly labeling the U.S. a Christian country. I think we can say, however, that the laws and practices of our nation reflect a general consensus on certain shared values —values that are in accordance with the Judeo-Christian ethic.

I think Aleksander Solzhenitsyn's commencement address at Harvard University in 1978 is a good starting point for understanding what I'm talking about. His central premise was that Western democracies have lost their way. We have forgotten that with freedom comes responsibility and accountability.

We have replaced a system of freedom and accountability

with a system of license and what Solzhenitsyn calls "moral mediocrity." Unbridled capitalism is clearly preferable to any form of communism or socialism. But a system whose only norms are determined by the marketplace or by the courtroom is, as he puts it, "not quite worthy of man."

I would like to believe, as Solzhenitsyn said, that we have reached a turning point in U.S. history. There is no golden age to which I want to return. But there is also no reason to be content with the present state of affairs. I hope for a future in which my children will have boundless opportunities to create and produce, but in which they will always be mindful of their accountability to God and their fellow man. We have made progress since 1980 toward greater freedom and prosperity. But I am not sure we have made corresponding progress toward freedom with accountability.

We have heard a lot recently, from liberals especially, about the separation of Church and state. They are even using this battle cry as a campaign issue to scare voters. Orthodox religions, for them, have become bogeymen to be flayed at every possible opportunity.

Separation of church and state, however, is not a constitutional provision. It is a refined version of the phrase Jefferson used in a letter to a friend in which he argued the need for a "wall of separation" between church and state. The Constitution provides for religious freedom and forbids Congress from establishing a national religion.

The provision that there be no national religion means that no one denomination will hold sway as, for example, the Anglican church does in England. Separation of church and state properly understood (if that is possible after all the anti-religious vitriol of recent years) allows great latitude for state cooperation and accommodation of religious organizations. Read Robert Cord's *Separation of Church and State: Historical Fact and Current Fiction* for the full story.

PETER FERRARA: As a Christian myself, I say, that it is wrong to call the U.S. a Christian country, because this can too easily be taken to mean that non-Christians do not have equal legal status with Christians. While Christians should be free to practice and pursue their religion in public as well as in private, America is not for Christians only. To call the U.S. a Christian country is highly offensive to Jews and other religious minorities.

It is important to add, however, that the term "separation of Church and state," evoked so passionately these days by liberals, appears nowhere in the Constitution. The phrase is used to explain the Constitution's Establishment Clause, which prohibits the federal government, and (by an erroneous judicial decision), state governments from "establishing" a religion.

The Founding Fathers intended by the Establishment Clause to codify what may be termed a "no preference" doctrine with regard to religion. That is, the government could aid religion if the people wanted, but if it did, it must aid all equally, without any preference for one over the other.

The official liberal interpretation of the Establishment Clause, however, can be designated as the "no aid" doctrine. That is, the government is prohibited from aiding religion in any way. Expansively interpreted, as the liberals prefer, "aid" can be considered as simply permitting any religious activity or expression in the public sector. By logical extension, religion must then be banned from the public schools, parks, streets, and "public" airwaves. This results in an egregious restriction of religious liberty, made all the more severe as the public sector grows.

A perfectly acceptable modern interpretation of the Establishment Clause can be designated as the "no discrimination" doctrine. That is, the government would be prohibited from discriminating in favor of or against religion. This doctrine would allow religion in the public sector on the same terms as every other form of expression or viewpoint, even though religion may benefit as a result. It would allow government aid to go to religion as long as the aid was part of a general government program with a secular purpose providing aid to more than just religious individuals and institutions. The religious should be permitted, in other words, to participate on the same terms as everyone else.

For example, tuition tax credits or vouchers for all schools, public or private, would be acceptable under this doctrine, even though private religious schools might also benefit. By allowing religious individuals and institutions the same privileges and rights as everyone else, how could there possibly be the "establishment" of a religion?

Through this no discrimination doctrine, virtually all church-state controversies today could be solved to the satisfaction of religious conservatives, and on grounds that should appeal across the whole political spectrum.

Chapter Six

ROLLING BACK THE EVIL EMPIRE

THE NATURE OF THE SOVIET THREAT

There was no greater unanimity of opinion than on the nature of the Soviet threat and on what should be the main objective of U.S. foreign policy. Every Third Generation participant sees the Soviet Union as the major menace to the survival of democracy and freedom in the world. Thus, the primary aim of U.S. foreign policy should be the liberation of Soviet-controlled territory, thereby rolling back rather than containing Moscow's gains. The following are some representative statements made both in formal presentations and by members of the audience.

PETER FERRARA: A conflict exists between the United States and the Soviet Union on a moral plane, apart from the military conflict. The United States represents the summit of Western civilization and its highly developed moral system with equality under the law, due process of law, human rights, individual dignity, autonomy, and freedom. The Soviet Union is a retrograde slave society, negating every moral principle of Western civilization—no equality under the law, no due process of law, no human rights, no respect for the dignity, autonomy, or freedom of the individual. The Soviet Union is wrong down to its conceptual roots in theory as well as practice. It is the moral equivalent of Nazi Germany.

This moral conflict is extended into a military conflict because the Soviet Union seeks world domination. This does not stem from historic Russian paranoia, but rather is a natural outgrowth of the Soviet ideology and system. Ideologically, the communists are driven to destroy the competing alternative—democratic capitalism. This is even more true since the obvious moral superiority of the West undermines the communists merely by contrast.

Systematically, the collectivist Soviet system, based on a centralized structure, in effect, imbues all aspects of society with a militarist caste. Leaders who claw their way to the top of such a society naturally think in terms of domination and militarism. Expansionism is also the only real means for the unproductive Soviet system to gain wealth, is used to justify domestic domination, and is viewed as a means of proving the superiority of the Soviet system and ideology.

There are no common goals, values, or aspirations between the West and the Soviet Union, that might form a basis for the reconciliation of this conflict.

GREGORY FOSSEDAL: Most conservatives, and many liberals, would now agree there can be only one goal: a democratic government in the Soviet Union. Marxism and democracy are irreconcilable systems. The Soviet elite cannot tolerate the existence of free nations that illustrate how despotic the Soviet government is and that hold out the promise of liberation. It follows, we must win or die. The Soviet elite can allow no other outcome.

A few years ago, this was regarded as a remarkably hawkish position. "You can't change the Soviet system," is but one of the assorted clichés that neatly sum up the regnant ethos. Today, even though the West has yet to achieve a major rollback, the climate seems altered. For one thing, 19 of 22 countries in Latin America are now democratic, as Adam Meyerson of *Policy Review* has pointed out, with Cuba and Nicaragua the notable exceptions and with Chile being the only non-communist nation that is also non-democratic, proving, in effect, that Jeane Kirkpatrick was right. Authoritarian regimes, she says, are distinct from totalitarian regimes in that they can readily become democratic. For all the American Left's hatred of Franco, he did, after all, move Spain, traditionally an authoritarian country, in a decidedly democratic direction. . . .

MICHAEL JOHNS: Our conflict with the Soviets is not purely one of philosophy or ideology. Rather, it is a conflict over their global expansionism and imperialism. The Soviet leadership has all but abandoned socialism in the ideological sense in favor of a civilization based around internal and external militarism. After all, there are other communist countries, such as Yugoslavia, that are also based on perverted and failing ideologies wholly contrary to ours. Our conflict with them has been minimal, however, because they are not an expansionist force. The Soviets, on the other hand, have repeatedly used and combined terrorism and violence and have disregarded any respect for moral behavior in the pursuit of their global aspirations. They are a force far more ruthless, ambitious, and barbaric than any the world has ever seen.

MICHAEL WALLER: The nature of the conflict between the United States and the Soviet Union is an ideological struggle for survival. The two diametrically opposed systems cannot coexist forever, and in the long run one system must be destroyed or incorporated into the other. The differences are irreconcilable.

While most U.S. leaders have been willing, even eager, to coexist with communism, the Soviet Union has steadily made gains since 1917. The Soviet leadership has stated its goal of destroying our system, and their actions betray any conciliatory words to the contrary. Only one player can win. And we are not winning. We can never succeed until we view the Soviets the way the Soviets view us: as enemies.

It is silly to speak of future wars with the USSR until we recognize that the Soviets declared war on our country, our system, and our values long ago. The West continues to give the Soviets the means with which to wage that war, which they can win without resorting to nuclear weapons.

A look at the map shows how that war has forced us farther and farther into retreat. Soviet strategy is aimed at capturing nations rich in natural resources or countries that skirt strategic sea lanes, such as the Persian Gulf, South Africa, Chile, Cuba, and Central America. In recent years, the Soviets have stepped up their efforts to force the United States to focus on its own borders at the expense of other parts of the world. Putting the U.S. on the defensive at its southern border through Mexico is not a strategy unique to the Soviets—it was attempted earlier in this century. Kaiser Wilhelm of Germany tried to do this in 1917 in order to keep the U.S. from joining the Allies in World War I. The Zimmermann telegram, which revealed the German plot to invade the U.S. through Mexico, should have taught us a lesson about what Stalin later referred to as our "strategic reserve."

Stalin noted in 1921: "If Europe and America may be called a front—the scene of the main engagements between socialism and imperialism—the non-sovereign nations and colonies with their raw materials, fuel, food and vast store of human material should be regarded as the rear, the reserve of imperialism. In order to win a war, one must not only triumph at the front, but also revolutionize the enemy's rear, his reserves." By drawing us into a war in Central America, and eventually tying us down in Mexico, the Soviets hope to render us helpless to protect our interests elsewhere.

Simultaneously, the Soviets exploit America's weaknesses through propaganda and disinformation, which blur the truth. For them, information is not a means to discern truth, it is another weapon with which to fight the West. The most effective lies are often those that come closest to the truth, and it is the manufacture of such lies that the Soviet propaganda machinery has mastered, which so often appear in the U.S. news media, presented as objective reporting.

PATRICK MCGUIGAN: The modern struggle between the U.S. and the Soviet Union is the latest installment of the age-old struggle between those who strive, however imperfectly, for good on the one hand and, on the other hand, those who strive for raw power and domination over the world. In essence, it is the human equivalent of the battle between God and his enemies. In the cosmic scheme of things, the good must prevail, but this is no guarantee that we will prevail over the Soviet Union.

It is important, of course, to recognize that America is not always right. But it is certainly true that we are usually on the right side and that our enemies are on the wrong side. We are as fallible as any nation, or any man, striving for righteousness. As Solzhenitsyn wrote in *The Gulag Archipelago*: "It became clear to me that the line separating good from evil runs not between states, not between classes, and not between parties—it runs through the heart of each and every one of us, and through all human hearts. The line is not stationary. It shifts and moves with the passage of the years. Even in hearts enveloped by evil, it maintains a small bridgehead of good. And even the most virtuous heart harbors an uprooted corner of evil."

A CONSERVATIVE FOREIGN POLICY

The tide of history has begun to move against the Soviet Union, largely because of the way in which people are treated when they fall under Moscow's subjugation. But history has also shown that the American people are not willing to undertake a sustained effort to roll back communism on their own. Moreover, direct military action on the part of the U.S. tends to stir up anti-American sentiments within the very nations we attempt to liberate. It is far better, in most instances, to assist existing indigenous anti-communist movements and take advantage of hostility that has developed within the communist bloc toward the Soviet presence. This strategy has come to be called "The Reagan Doctrine" and represents something of a shift in conservative thinking.

PETER FERRARA: The primary goal of U.S. foreign policy should be to maintain the security and freedom of the American people. This means, of course, avoiding nuclear war, but also resisting Soviet world domination, which is a threat to our freedom and security.

Containment is a failure. The U.S. must seek to roll back Soviet influence wherever possible. This means first and foremost banishing the Soviets from the Western Hemisphere. We must then seek to roll back Soviet domination wherever else it appears to be weakening, for instance in Angola and Mozambique. Ultimately, we must hope to some day have the opportunity to free Russia itself from communism. This policy is correct and justifiable not only on national security grounds but on moral grounds as well.

Michael Johns: Our long-range goal should be the worldwide promulgation and eventual triumph of freedom and democracy. The U.S. must recognize itself as one of the few benevolent and moral forces in the world. It also must realize, in the words of Anwar Sadat, that "if America does not lead the free world, then the free world will have no leader." We must now come to the aid of those democratic states who are opposing Soviet-backed dictatorships and attempt to educate, through programs such as Radio Marti, those who are forced to live under Soviet-style communism. America must go beyond containment and make its long-term goal victory over communism. To accomplish this, we need to overhaul our State Department and foreign service so that it will commit itself, over the long haul, to worldwide democratic victory.

Our immediate objective must be strengthening and preparing our allies for the war that is being waged upon democracy. Before discarding Chile or South Africa to some hostile power, we ought to remember what happened when we undermined the Shah of Iran, Fulgencio Batista in Cuba, and Anastasio Somoza in Nicaragua. We must provide the aid and training necessary for our allies to protect themselves because, unlike the Soviet Union, America's democratic political system will not allow the U.S. to fight on a dozen different fronts.

Frank Lavin: The proper conduct of foreign policy is to reconcile our goals in the international arena with our capabilities. The Soviets understand this, which is why they are always searching for, and finding, targets of opportunity. The United States would do well to adopt this strategy and use it to topple communist governments. There would virtually never be any need for direct U.S. military involvement, only a willingness to support anti-communist guerrillas. . . .

We should support the "moderately repressive authoritarian governments," as Jeane Kirkpatrick calls them, when the most likely alternative would be worse, be it Marxist or something along the lines of what the Ayatollah has established. We should oppose authoritarian, Somoza-style governments when it appears there is an organized democratic alternative ready to step in. Even when we support a nondemocratic authoritarian regime, we must take special care to support democratic opposition elements in the country, including political parties, trade unions, religious organizations, the media, and business and civic groups. This is both a moral and tactical necessity. Morally, our support for democratic organizations allows us to demonstrate to the particular government that we disapprove of its regime and seek to improve it. Tactically, this preempts a nondemocratic opposition from co-opting legitimate reform movements.

MICHAEL WALLER: To fight the Soviet threat, we need not introduce our own military forces into combat. The U.S. should invest its resources in undermining the Soviet empire from within. Trade embargoes against Moscow and its client states, stepped-up broadcasting of the Voice of America and Radio Free Europe, and exploiting the many racial and cultural tensions within the USSR must be pursued vigorously and, if possible, in concert with our allies.

It is a moral imperative to aid the thousands of Nicaraguans, Angolans, Afghans, Mozambicans, Ethiopians, Cambodians, Laotians, Vietnamese, and other oppressed peoples who will do the fighting if only we give them the means with which to fight. As long as we help these people fight their own wars themselves, not a single American life need be lost. On the other hand, if we stand idly by, we will still have no choice in the future but to send in American military personnel as a last, desperate resort. Then Americans will be sent to die in wars that our national leaders were too timid and indecisive to have prevented when they had the chance.

Meanwhile, we should do all we can to encourage the mainland Chinese when they denounce Soviet aggression. A billion unfriendly Chinese as neighbors makes the Soviets nervous and ties up enormous military resources that would otherwise be directed toward Western Europe or the United States.

HOW CONSERVATIVE IS REAGAN'S FOREIGN POLICY?

There was wide disagreement over whether there has, in fact, been a Reagan Revolution in foreign policy. The following excerpts from statements by Third Generation members illustrate the differences in opinion that marked the discussions.

ADAM MEYERSON: Ronald Reagan has reinvigorated the NATO alliance; he has built up U.S. defense capabilities; he has championed strategic defense; and he has repealed the Brezhnev Doctrine with his rescue of Grenada. He is the first president in recent years to call the Soviets what they are—an evil empire. His principal mistake is that he has not focused enough public attention on the Soviet military threat. Americans and other democratic peoples should be reminded over and over just how many tanks and missiles the Soviets are brandishing. Otherwise we will follow our natural inclinations and ignore our defenses.

Only under rare circumstances should the United States use its own troops. But we must abide by our treaty commitments to come to the aid of allies attacked by the Soviet bloc. We also are obliged to defend any country in our hemisphere invaded by Cuba, Nicaragua, or any other Soviet ally.

Our Grenada operation was a wise use of force. Neighboring islands, terrified by the Soviet and Cuban build-up in Grenada, asked us to intervene. We acted decisively and with sufficient power so that we were able to win quickly with very limited American casualties. And although we appeared to much of the world to be interfering in Grenada's internal affairs, the Grenadians universally welcomed us as liberators.

The emergence of anti-communist guerrilla forces in Afghanistan, Cambodia, Mozambique, Angola, and Nicaragua is one of the most important political developments of our times. Not only has the romance of revolution shifted from the communists to the anti-communists, but the Soviet empire is now on the defensive, with more than territory at stake. At issue is the single most important question in the politics of ideology: Who owns the future? When anti-communist guerrillas start overthrowing communist tyrannies, then worldwide communist victory can no longer be considered inevitable.

If an anti-communist resistance force asks us for help, we should give it, provided the freedom fighters have strong popular support in their country. Normally, it would not be the business of the United States to seek the overthrow of a foreign government. But the Soviets and their allies have been trying to overthrow legitimate governments for years, and the Soviets violate international law every day with their occupation of Eastern Europe. We should not be constrained by international law in our policy toward outlaw nations.

GREGORY FOSSEDAL: Ten years ago the national liberation movements around the world were both anti-colonialist and anti-Western. For this reason, in the eyes of many, the anti-communists seemed to be on the moral defensive.

Today, the climate has changed. The national liberation movements are still anti-colonialist, but now they are also anti-Soviet. This is an historic turn of events, because it means that we don't need to use U.S. military power, as we did in Vietnam, to pursue a rollback policy against Moscow's foreign policy designs. We need only give sanction and support to existing indigenous movements fighting against Soviet colonial control.

Thus, we assume the moral high ground by encouraging anti-colonial movements without becoming involved directly. As a result, for very little expense, the U.S. has a chance simultaneously to promote the cause of freedom, serve U.S. interests, confound Moscow's foreign policy, and win the affections of the people of the Third World who are tired of being constantly overrun by outside superpowers.

Some liberation movements will succeed, others will fail. But at least we will be able to say with honesty that America was on the side of freedom and national sovereignty and that we did not treat smaller countries as the Soviets do, that is, as pawns on a chessboard.

Michael Waller: We have had no significant long-term successes in foreign policy with respect to the Soviet Union since World War II, unless one shamelessly considers mere containment of the USSR an end in itself.

President Reagan is the best president we have had in this century, but he has allowed his conservative agenda to be undermined not only by the State Department bureaucracy, but by many of the people he appointed himself. His efforts in Central America and Grenada have been admirable, but his policies toward the rest of the developing world, for example Africa, differ little from those of Jimmy Carter. President Reagan has spared no bluster in responding to Soviet provocations, but in practice he has been very weak in response to such atrocities as the shooting down of the Korean airliner, the murder of Major Nicholson, and other similar instances. President Reagan is extremely popular. He should use his last years in office to mobilize the American people in an all-out offensive against the Soviet empire and the Soviet system itself.

MICHAEL JOHNS: Since President Reagan has come to office, there have been three Soviet initiatives that have warranted tough responses: the murder of Major Nicholson in Berlin, the shooting down of the Korean passenger plane, flight KAL 007, over the Sakhalin Islands, and the deployment of assault helicopters in Marxist Nicaragua. In all three instances, the Reagan response has consisted almost entirely of harsh rhetoric. Aid and trade with the Soviets should have been cut off promptly after the KAL 007 massacre. The message we sent to the Soviets by not acting was that we would tolerate such actions. Had we responded to the shooting down of the airliner, the murder of Major Nicholson might not have occurred, because the Soviets would have understood that we are serious about protecting our people and our interests. . . .

The appointment of Chester Crocker to the position of Assistant Secretary of State for African Affairs was a major blunder. Crocker has consolidated the communist dictatorship of Mozambique by, first, undercutting the Renamo freedom fighters who were close to toppling the brutal Soviet-installed Mozambique regime and, second, putting together a policy of actually propping up that Marxist dictatorship through $27 million in aid. Crocker also has done his best to sell out the Angolan freedom fighters in their bid to topple the Soviet-installed regime in Luanda. In addition, he has pressured South Africa to withdraw its support for pro-democratic movements in Mozambique and Angola.

The Reagan Administration, following the advice of the Department of State, has failed to put sufficient economic pressure on the Soviets. For example, following the Soviet invasion of Afghanistan in December 1979, Carter imposed 13 sanctions on the Soviets, some very strong, including the grain embargo, the Olympic boycott, severing of diplomatic relations with Kabul, tighter restrictions on credit and technology transfers, a severance of cultural exchanges. All these sanctions have been lifted under Reagan.

When we offer the Soviets favorable economic arrangements, technology, credit, below-market prices for our goods and services, we allow them to devote more resources to their massive military build-up, intelligence and disinformation networks, and the propping up and financing of anti-Western dictators and revolutionaries. Thus, when Lenin said that the capitalists "will sell us the rope with which to hang them," he understated his case. We are selling them the rope on credit, for less than it costs us to make it.

FRANK LAVIN: Reagan's single greatest foreign policy achievement, without a doubt, was the liberation of Grenada. Admittedly, this was more a symbolic than a substantive victory. But it marked the first genuine rollback of Soviet imperialism. It also served as a reminder to Americans that, distasteful as conflict is, the use of troops is sometimes the only way to defend our ideals of liberty and democracy. In addition, the successful use of American troops helped reforge a consensus among the general public that there are times when the use of the American military abroad makes sense. That, in itself, can be a boon to the conduct of U.S. foreign policy, as it strengthens our credibility with our friends, as well as our adversaries.

Now, public support for using a few thousand troops for a few days of low-intensity conflict hardly shows that Americans would support an interventionist or militaristic foreign policy, nor should conservatives welcome such a development. It does indicate, however, that the public is moving away from the dangerously isolationist sentiment of the 1970s.

THE MIDDLE EAST

There was virtual unanimity among Third Generation speakers that Israel is the West's strongest ally in the Middle East and that its protection should be a principal aim of U.S. policy in that region. This view marks a shift from the position of many conservatives from previous generations who viewed Israel's emergence with scepticism. As a result of this change in thinking, many American Jewish intellectuals, once on the Left, have moved into the conservative camp. Meanwhile, sentiment against supporting Israel has percolated to the top of the agenda of many liberals. Jesse Jackson vehemently opposes U.S. support of Israel, and his presence influenced the Democratic platform in the 1984 presidential campaign. The Democratic platform did not, for example, include combating anti-Semitism in its long list of civil rights objectives. Moreover, the Democratic Party did not insist that Jackson repudiate one of his major supporters, Louis Farrakhan, for his favorable comments about Hitler. As a result, an increasing number of American Jews are arriving at the conclusion that the real anti-Semitism is on the Left.

ADAM MEYERSON: Together with Turkey, Israel is the only genuine ally of the United States in the Middle East. It is a democracy; it is a land of political and religious freedom;

it is the most humane country in the region. Israel's enemies are our enemies, particularly Syria, the Palestine Liberation Organization, Libya, and Iranian fanaticism. And Israel's military victories have been for Western strategic interests and Western political values.

MICHAEL WALLER: Israel's role in U.S. foreign policy is three-fold: First, we are helping fulfill a Biblical prophecy by supporting Israel. Support for Israel, thus, becomes a decidedly Christian act. Second, we are safeguarding the human rights of the Jewish people, who have been persecuted for thousands of years and who finally have a homeland of their own. They govern the only democracy in the Middle East. Third, we are enhancing our own national security interests since Israel is the most potent military presence in the Middle East. In addition, Israel appears to be the only Judeo-Christian country willing to act swiftly and decisively to repel its enemies. Israel is our most valuable ally, because it seems to be the only democratic nation in the world willing to do what it takes to survive, unfortunately often to its detriment in the eyes of world opinion, which has the unique capacity to change the behavior of only the free nations.

MICHAEL JOHNS: The Middle East is no stranger to anti-American sentiments and, consequently, we need Israel to remain a strong ally. Historically, Israel has served as a defender of American interests in the region. In 1970, Israel mobilized to defend moderate Jordan from Syrian attack. Israeli intelligence has frequently warned the U.S. and other Arab allies of impending actions against them by terrorists such as the Libyans and Iranian Shi'ites. The Israelis drove two Soviet proxies, the Syrians and the PLO, from Beirut and opened Lebanon to the U.S. Our State Department, by waffling on support for Israel, has since made a shambles of U.S. policy there, but that is not Israel's fault.

We must make it clear to Israel, however, that although we will not allow a defensive breakdown of the country, we also will not tolerate the economic disaster brought on by their socialist-leaning economic structure. We are committing a lot of money to Israel, much of which is going down a socialist rat hole. We must encourage them to shape up their economy, cut domestic spending, and eliminate price subsidies. Israeli government expenditures now consume more than 60 percent of their entire GNP and threaten to plunge the country into Third World status by strangling its productive capability.

Chapter Seven

DISMANTLING THE WELFARE STATE

RATING REAGAN'S PERFORMANCE

President Reagan's tenure in office has proved how difficult it is to cut the size of government. Once an agency is in place, it is virtually impossible to eliminate it. Domestic spending has actually increased under the Reagan Presidency, even though the foremost theme of his 1980 campaign against President Carter was a promise to reduce federal expenditures and to get government off the backs of the people. Peter Ferrara's comments are representative of conservative frustrations expressed at the Third Generation forums.

PETER FERRARA: President Reagan's greatest shortcoming has been the failure to reduce government spending. His next greatest has been the failure to adopt basic monetary reform, involving a modernized version of the gold standard and instead allowing the Federal Reserve Board to damage economic performance severely and unnecessarily.

Another major problem has been the failure to appoint individuals committed to conservative policies to all key positions in the Administration. This failure ruined whole major categories of domestic policy. The single worst appointment of Reagan's Presidency was Terrell Bell as Education Secretary. Bell took a mandate to abolish the Department of Education and turned it into a successful campaign for sharp increases in public education spending at the state and local levels, while maintaining the Department. The appointment of William Bennett to succeed Bell has been a dramatic improvement, but much time has been lost.

The President has also failed to deregulate sufficiently. The Interstate Commerce Commission should have been abolished; environmental regulation should have been thoroughly overhauled; civil rights laws should have been revised to provide explicitly for a colorblind society; Davis-Bacon, the minimum wage law, and many other regulations should have been addressed more vigorously.

WHAT SHOULD GOVERNMENT DO?

All conservatives agree that government should not be involved in anywhere near the number of areas it is today. There was some disagreement over exactly how far the public sector should be scaled back. Opinion ranged from the position that government should be about half the size it is now to the view that government should virtually disappear.

PETER FERRARA: I would not object to government providing police, laws, courts, prisons, roads, bridges, public parks, fire protection, and national defense. The public also demands a minimum government welfare system to provide basic essentials to those truly in need. Some regulation regarding environmental protection and public safety is justified. Everything else the government does is a counterproductive mistake and/or a grave injustice, and/or something that can be done better by the private sector.

There may be some other truly public goods that only government can provide, but I cannot think of any. Arguments for increasing government intervention are generally fraudulent.

Even in those areas where I find the presence of government acceptable, the private sector can often supplement it to a large extent, if not supplant it entirely. For example, police can be supplemented by private security guards, courts by private arbitration, and applicable law in a commercial setting by contractual agreement, all of which are often the case today. Local roads are sometimes provided by affected property owners. Bridges and interstate roads could be constructed by private, toll-charging companies, and the U.S. infrastructure would probably be in better shape if they were. Fire protection and prisons can be contracted out. Environmental protection could be supplanted by more rigorously defined property rights and broader application of nuisance laws. Private charity often does a better job than government welfare.

PATRICK MCGUIGAN: In theory, there is a proper role for government intervention in the economy when it is operating unfairly to the advantage of the big boys: the international banks, big corporations, and other such interests.

It is the practice of government regulation that has convinced me that my own presuppositions (about the legitimacy of government action) are faulty. It is hard for me to accept the *laissez faire* economic model as adequate for a just society. Yet in practice it seems the best system. A free economy promotes many of the stated goals of those who make the theoretical case for government intervention.

The present economic system in America, however, is so

hopelessly skewed with a variety of disincentives and nonincentives that those of us on the Right should be willing to abolish many existing programs outright. I lean heavily toward the concept that the lowest level of government in combination with the private sector should deal with social problems. These days, everything seems to be a federal case. I utterly reject the implicit message of the American Bishops' pastoral letter on the economy. That is a radical departure from the things I was taught about social justice as a child.

PETER YOUNG: I firmly believe that conservatives should attempt to stamp out government wherever it occurs, with but few exceptions, such as national defense, police, and perhaps one or two other areas.

The reason for my position should be known to everyone. When the private and public sectors are compared, one finds that services performed by the government cost on average 40 percent more than if done by the private sector. The public sector is less efficient, requires more manpower to carry out its tasks, and has no consumer input to determine what it ought to be producing, because it has no competition. The government is not required to make a profit in order to stay in business. Moreover, its objective is, quite simply, to remain in power; thus decisions made in the public sector are determined by electoral considerations rather than economics.

Not only is government far more expensive to operate than private business, its methods are notoriously shoddy, inflexible, and unresponsive to the demands of the public. Most of the big service interruptions during Prime Minister Thatcher's term in Great Britain have been in publicly owned industries: coal strikes, postal strikes, health workers' strikes, and so on. Now, these industries were nationalized, in theory, to ensure uninterrupted service. But precisely the opposite has happened.

I am convinced that government prevents progress, creates poverty rather than prosperity, and is a public nuisance. Therefore, as many government functions as possible should be moved immediately to the private sector.

CAN CONSERVATIVES CUT SPENDING AND WIN POLITICALLY?

All Third Generation participants agree that President Reagan's failure to reduce domestic spending does not stem from a lack of desire on his part to do so. We find instead that, whenever the President proposes to eliminate a single dollar from nondefense public expenditures, he comes under vicious attack from Congress, the media, and special interest lobbies. The Administration has so far proved no match for this opposition. The result has been not only the failure to reduce the scope of government, but an actual increase in its total domestic budget. Both Peter Ferrara, a former senior staffer on Policy Development at the White House, and Peter Young, director of the Adam Smith Institute's Washington office, argue that the President has failed in this area because he has pursued the wrong strategy.

PETER FERRARA: At least half of federal spending, two-thirds of state and local spending, and the great bulk of federal, state, and local regulations are unnecessary, mostly on grounds that a majority of Americans would find acceptable.

But the Reagan Administration's budget-cutting approach has been all wrong. It has sought simple, flat-out cuts in programs, largely on overall fiscal policy grounds. It has not emphasized at all fundamental reforms that would allow the generally laudable goals of these programs to be accomplished with much less government spending, either through the private sector or through totally restructured government programs.

One fundamental theme of such structural reform is privatization. This involves reforms that allow functions currently provided by government to be performed through the private sector. At the federal level, the greatest potential for this strategy involves the otherwise untouchable Social Security and Medicare programs. Workers can be given a simple option to substitute expanded Individual Retirement Accounts (IRAs) for at least part, and then eventually all, of their Social Security retirement benefits. They could be allowed to purchase life and disability insurance through their IRAs as substitutes for Social Security's survivors and disability insurance. They could be allowed to save extra IRA funds for retirement medical insurance in substitution for Medicare. In this way, federal spending could be reduced by as much as 30 percent, without any benefit cuts at all, by workers themselves choosing on an individual basis a better deal in the private sector.

Also at the federal level, public housing programs can be privatized by turning over ownership of existing projects to the tenants and granting housing vouchers to new tenants, which will allow them to purchase their own housing in the private sector. The Federal Aviation Administration can be privatized as a corporation performing its services to the private aviation industry for a fee. Public television and public radio can be privatized as commercial networks. Federal lands, currently used by private commercial interests, can be sold to those users.

Privatization has even greater possibilities at the state and local levels. Many state and local services can be taken over entirely by private companies, such as hospital and utility services. The greatest potential at the state and local level is in the area of education. First, private schooling is demonstrably better than public education. Consequently, parents should be granted the option to choose private rather than public schools through tuition tax credits and education vouchers. This would be of particular benefit to the poor. Instead of having their children trapped in a bad school in the inner city, poor parents could take their voucher, the equivalent of money, and use it to go to their choice of private school. There is hardly a single state or local government activity that cannot be contracted out to a private firm by the state or local government itself.

More fertile ground for structural reform is the welfare system. The numerous, overlapping welfare efforts at the federal, state, and local levels should be thoroughly overhauled and rationalized. The new system could provide funds to the truly needy, as the public demands, with an enormous cost reduction at the same time by eliminating waste, overlapping payments, subsidies to those not truly in need, and the enormous disincentives of the current system.

The New Federalism, as outlined by President Reagan early in his Administration, could bring about perhaps the most profound reform in government. Much federal spending is for functions that could be handled by state and local authorities. Voters at the state and local levels would be better able to scrutinize this spending and determine if they really wanted it. President Reagan should begin to emphasize this theme again.

In addition, cuts in federal pay scales and retirement benefits and in big business subsidies should be pursued with more vigor. But even here, fundamental reform would help as well. Replacing civilian and military pensions with federal contributions to expanded IRAs for each worker would eliminate cost of living adjustments and early retirement problems. Veterans' benefits for new recruits should be replaced with up front aid, such as education and training assistance, more meaningful to such young recruits, but far less costly in the long run.

Each of these themes not only reduces government spending, while still providing the same services that voters want, but also results in better service. Privatization usually means more efficiency, lower cost, and better quality. IRAs can provide better and higher benefits for today's young workers than Social Security. Welfare reform can eliminate waste and disincentives while delivering aid to those truly in need. This New Federalism can give voters greater control over programs.

PETER YOUNG: I would argue that all the hubbub over the departure of David Stockman and the charges that appeared in his subsequent book about the Reagan Administration's inability to get spending under control are painfully redundant. No American administration has been able to get spending under control because they have always attempted to cut costs in the wrong way. President Reagan would do well, I think, to follow the strategy of Margaret Thatcher, who has made considerable progress in scaling back the public sector.

The strategy of which I speak is called privatization. We at the Adam Smith Institute maintain that the only possible way to reduce the cost of government is to reduce its size. The Reagan Administration and subsequent administrations need to institute an ongoing program to transfer government functions to the private sector.

Now, we know this strategy works, because it has been tried and tested in Great Britain. In 1979, the Conservative Party's manifesto, an agenda for the Thatcher Administration, did not actually mention the word privatization. It talked about waste, and imposing cash limits on government programs, and managing them more efficiently, and so forth. It was quickly evident that this did not work very effectively. So privatization was really adopted in 1981 and since then has been gathering speed.

The list of things that have been privatized in Britain includes British railway hotels, English Channel ferry services, British Petroleum, British Aerospace, Cable and Wireless, Associated British Ports, Jaguar cars, the National Freight Corporation, several shipyards, Hoverspeed, one million public sector houses, British Telecom, Royal ordnance factories, Gibraltar dockyards, land and buildings belonging to a variety of public sector institutions, and parts of state-owned forests. There has been widespread contracting out of services by local authorities, including a variety of government services run by state hospitals, the maintenance and cleaning of government buildings, the testing of trucks and public vehicles, the laundry and cleaning services used by the military, and even the cleaning of restrooms at London's Kings Cross Railroad station. The largest current privatization effort is British Gas, the largest ever flotation on the London Stock Exchange worth about $8 billion, which will be followed by British Airways and the British Airports Authority, which owns all the large airports in Britain.

The conventional wisdom in the U.S. is that Britain has sold only state-owned industries, and because the U.S. does not have many of those, privatization can be conveniently forgotten here. I think this conventional wisdom is wrong. Privatization is not just about selling off state-owned industries. It seeks to have all public operations handled privately. It is a systematic campaign to replace the public sector with the private sector in all of its forms.

This can be done in the area of health care, Social Security, education, and even the regulatory function of government. In Britain, we are making progress on all these fronts. We have made more progress on state-owned industries because there are more of them and they are easier to change.

Norman Tebbit, Chairman of the Conservative Party in Britain, and the chap who is most likely to succeed Mrs. Thatcher as leader of the Party, has said that in 1979 Britain had the largest public sector of any Western economy, and that by 1990, it will have the smallest. I think he is right.

Let me give you some examples of four current privatization moves in Britain, which have relevance for the U.S. The first is Social Security. The Thatcher government has passed legislation to privatize the upper level of the British version of Social Security, called SERPS, which some people think is a social disease. It stands for the State Earnings Related Pensions Scheme, and it is an addition to the basic pension that everyone receives and is related to earnings. Some time ago the government gave people the right to opt out of this scheme and take a private pension instead. Now, by 1986, over half of the population has done so, and this has made it considerably easier to further privatize the system, because political support for SERPS has been undermined.

The government has now moved to phase out SERPS and encourage everyone to take a private pension. You might think that this would create a great fuss. But, in fact, there is little complaint because so many people have opted out of the system already. Also the phasing out of SERPS will, to a certain extent, be gradual. That is, all those over 45 will be able to remain in SERPS if they so wish. Therefore, all the main potential opposition has been accommodated. The Labor Party is very upset about it, but there is no mass of people opposing it, no demonstrations on the streets or anything like that.

I think America's Social Security system, which takes up half of the entire domestic spending budget, should use Britain's privatization of the SERPS system as a model.

Indeed, Peter Ferrara and various other people have put forth proposals that would get government out of the pension business quickly and painlessly. Privatization of Social Security is the only way, in fact, to get the U.S. government out of its deficit mess.

Another privatization move that is being undertaken by Thatcher, which I think has great application in this country, is compulsory tendering for local services. The Adam Smith Institute over the past five or six years has published a whole variety of publications urging the contracting out of local government services such as garbage collection, cleaning buildings, providing school meals, and that sort of thing.

Indeed, there have been widespread moves by a variety of local authorities who have taken this up, perhaps constituting about 10 percent of the total of such services and saving these local governments a lot of money. Now the government has accepted a key proposal, which is to make it compulsory for all such services that can be provided by private firms to be put out for tender and for the lowest bid to be accepted.

The list of services where tendering is required at present at the local level includes: street cleaning, cleaning of buildings, catering, vehicle maintenance, refuse collection, and grounds maintenance. Once this legislation is passed, the list can be expanded at the whim of the Secretary of State.

I think, once again, that this would be a profitable road for the U.S. to take. You, of course, have a much more decentralized political system. And among conservatives there is a great reluctance to allow the federal government to force the local governments to do things. On this sort of issue, it is worth using the power of the federal government to restrict the number of grants to local governments if they do not put services out for tender and if they do not get value for their money. One can look at the local government in a different way, as a kind of mafia with permission from the central authorities to extort money from the local taxpayers. And as conservatives, it is our duty to use the federal authority to prevent the extortion of money from the taxpayer by these local mafias, euphemistically called local governments.

The third area where we are making real progress in Britain is in the deregulation of local transport services. In 1980, the government introduced a bill to deregulate long distance bus service, with the result that fares dropped dramatically as competition for business increased. There is a bill now being put through the House of Commons which is going to remove all regulation of all bus services, meaning that anyone will be able to set up a bus service anywhere and run in competition with the present monopoly service either in town or in a rural area. Furthermore, the present bus services, owned and operated by the state, are being sold off to the private sector. Thus, we will have an entirely private and deregulated transport system with the exception of London, because the government, being politically realistic, does not want a fuss on the doorsteps of Parliament. So London is being exempted from the privatization effort, for the time being, until the rest of it goes through.

The fourth area, which I think is of particular interest to Americans, is the Post Office. Now, it is not yet an officially announced policy of the British government to privatize the Post Office, but it has been leaked to the newspapers that such a policy will shortly be announced.

A few years ago, the government broke up what was called the GPO, the General Post Office, into two sections: the Post Office, which handles letters and so forth, and British Telecom, the state-owned telephone service, which was sold, as you know, in 1984. Then the government allowed competition with the Post Office for letters costing more than one pound to deliver. A large number of private post office companies were set up. They are working very efficiently and reliably, and there have been no strikes in the postal service, because every time the government postal workers threaten to strike, the government threatens to lift the monopoly entirely, which they know would decimate the Post Office. So, predictably, there have been no strikes.

The government has split the Post Office function into four separate areas, which will be organized along company lines: the counter services, which are the actual post offices themselves, where you have to wait a half hour in line before you get anything done; the National Gyro Savings Bank (which is part of the postal operation in Britain); letter delivery; and parcel delivery.

Gyro Savings Bank will probably just be sold off on the stock market. The counter services, that is, the actual post offices themselves, will probably allow each post office to exist as a separate company, basically giving it to the employees there, who would contract with the central post office for supply of stamps and so forth. That way the Post Office could be sold off to some of the larger banks. Post office services would be subcontracted out to those or other retail outlets. Thus, there would be free competition in the delivery of mail. I think this is definitely in the cards.

Frankly, unless the Post Office is privatized, it is going to be made obsolete by advancing technology. Electronic mail is going to replace mail delivery within the next 25 years.

So these are four areas where Britain has made great gains in privatization, and where the U.S. can simply adapt the basic model for its own purposes. I would suggest that the Reagan Administration, and any future administration, adopt privatization as its main budget-cutting strategy.

First, raise the level of rhetoric and debate about privatization. President Reagan as well as the next president should make all sorts of speeches about it. People should be congratulated who have done it successfully on a local level. Local officials will then begin to fall over themselves to privatize everything because they know they will be recognized by the President for doing so. Second, effective privatization proposals must be carefully thought out. America is different from Britain, and the political obstacles are not quite the same. Adjustments must be made to accommodate the various vested interests who will oppose privatization.

It is important to understand that the genius of privatization is that it is popular. Good privatization proposals should always be popular. Britain's selling off of public housing to tenants at drastically reduced prices was wildly popular.

A privatization strategy for America would quickly solve U.S. deficit problems, not only because the costs of government would go down, but also because the government would raise a lot of money from asset sales. The reason many local as well as many central governments are in financial straits is that they have too many money-losing assets that they have to pay for, assets that could be transformed into money-making assets in the private sector. This is one of the reasons that the government in Britain is so keen on privatization: The government needs the money in order not to have to raise taxes. The situation has reached the point where the government has to privatize more and more things every year in order to keep the budget on an even keel.

Federal lands in the U.S. are alone worth more than the $200 billion budget deficit. And there are many other holdings and services owned by the U.S. government that are worth large sums of money. A lot of money could be raised quickly from asset sales. The budget deficit would be solved and government costs simultaneously reduced, because a lot of money is consumed in managing all these assets. Furthermore, by transferring government assets and functions to the private sector, the tax base is expanded, which means more potential for raising revenue or cutting taxes.

Such is the Adam Smith Institute's basic strategy for shrinking government. Of course, it will take a good deal of time to hammer out practical proposals in the U.S., but I will leave that up to you.

Chapter Eight

THE WAR IN THE TRENCHES

It is well and good to sit in Washington planning strategy and hammering out the fine points of political theory. But at some point someone must actually go out into the country and begin mobilizing the masses for action. Letters need to be written; protests needs to be organized; voters must be registered; and a whole range of issues at the state and local levels, many of which have a greater effect on the lives of individuals than decisions made in Washington, need to be addressed. Amy Moritz and Connie Heckman suggest actions that must be taken in these areas.

AMY MORITZ: As "true believers," it is our view that a conservative revolution is in the hearts and minds of the people. And we can afford no mistake: It is a revolution. Our job is not so much to preserve what is—although much of value requires preservation—but to regain control of our institutions, our government, and our courts. And the desire to regain control alone is not enough. Our leftist counterparts will not yield without a fight. To win, we need a strategy that is as simple to design as it is tedious to implement:

The War in the Trenches

- We must *locate* all potential conservative activists.
- We must *motivate* all potential activists to be activists.
- We must *train* all activists.
- We must *supply* all activists with the tools they need.

We must locate, motivate, train, and supply. And then we need to repeat the process, again and again. It is not an intellectual challenge; it is an organizational one.

The questions we must address are:

1) How successful have we been so far?
2) What are our current resources?
3) What are our next steps?

Just how successful have we been so far? Conservatives of the Third Generation must be grateful for the Second Generation's realization that conservatives must think in terms of "how to" rather than "what is." That is, the nuances of academic debate over public policy issues are only important when framed in the context of "how do we affect public policy?" Academics like to say: "Ideas have consequences." This is only partially true. An idea in a vacuum has no consequence. Only ideas that are acted upon do. And today, 50 years after the New Deal, 20 years after the Great Society, and after the formation of a tradition of foreign policy paralysis brought on by Vietnam and fine tuned into an institutionalized wimpishness by the Carter Administration, we cannot afford to have ideas that are merely acted upon—they must be acted upon fast, efficiently, and with dertermination.

But despite the successes of our elders, it was estimated at the last Third Generation gathering, by someone with far more Washington experience than I, that grass-roots conservative activism is only 50 to 70 percent what it was in

1979 to 1980. I do not have the experience to know if this figure is accurate. But if it is, we as a movement have become too complacent. We are too influenced by the fact that the building of a powerful, effective, grass-roots organization is difficult, time-consuming, and tedious. We have become impatient with the work of preliminary organization and are too anxious to reap the rewards. In short: If we do not improve our efforts, we will not succeed.

The second task is to evaluate our current resources, and here, the picture is not bleak. In my opinion, the conservative movement today is well-designed. The existence of numerous conservative groups rather than a single large organization prevents stagnation or a movement-wide accidental reliance upon an incorrect strategy. Competition can exist between organizations, and this works to encourage increased effectiveness. Strategies are considered for long-term as well as short-term goals. The movement has an adequate talent supply. In the long run we have adequate financial resources. Communication between organizations is regular. The movement's structure is sound: If each organization were to fulfill its self-assigned tasks we would have no jobs left undone.

On the other hand, our movement is weak in that our structural goals are not being met. Even our best organizations find that there is too much to do in too little time. Communication between organizations is not adequate to prevent some tasks from being done twice, while other tasks are not done at all. Our project selection is not always optimum. On the whole, however, a restructuring of the conservative movement is not called for. As Third Generation activists, we are greatly aided by our inheritance of an organizationally sound movement.

Again: Our task is to locate, motivate, train, and supply all possible activists. There are many points and strategies to consider. I will mention only a few.

1) We must develop idealistic reasons to motivate our conservative constituency. This is often referred to as "assuming the moral high ground." Negativism—that is, complaining about such things as the media or the establishment—works well as a motivator of short-term action but falls short as an influence for long-term activism. That is why negative "scare stories" work well for direct mail solicitation, but only because packages are designed to instigate immediate response. An example of activists motivated by idealism include those motivated by religious beliefs. Marxists use this tool well, and so should we.

2) Although in the motivation of long-term activists we must always strive for idealism, we must also keep in mind that idealism only exists after an individual's basic wants have been fulfilled. As capitalists, we should be the first to recognize the positive uses of self-interest. We can also personalize issues to make the potential activists feel as well as believe. For example, it is reported that prior to the Boston Massacre Sam Adams said that the optimum result of a civilian clash with the British would be four dead. Ten would be too many, he reasoned, because the event would be impersonal. Less than four would not be an adequate tragedy. But four or five would keenly affect the public. Five people were killed during the Boston Massacre—and the rest is history.

We can tailor Sam Adams's lesson to our times. If we read that the Sandinistas killed 5,000 people in their first few months of power, it does not affect us. When we see the pictures and personal stories of a few of these victims, we feel for them, and we want to help.

Another example is the Soviet Union's attack on the Korean airliner KAL 007. When 269 people are killed, we think in terms of what slogan to produce. Two-hundred-sixty-nine fits on a button or a bumper sticker. That's one reaction. But when we see shoes wash up on a beach in Japan and see the high school pictures from people's wallets, we have a real sense of the enormity of what has happened. We must design programs to make people actually feel the issues, which will be a much more useful motivating factor in the long run than simply an intellectual belief in the conservative viewpoint.

3) I also believe that, generally, people are not inclined to become political activists unless they believe they can do so without losing something in the process. They do not want to appear different from the other guy in the community. We must encourage such people to become activists by assuring them that they are not at risk of looking or behaving differently.

I suggest doing this very gradually. One way is to contact someone you know is a conservative and encourage him or her to become an activist by engaging him in activities that are similar to the kinds of things he is already doing. You could suggest to this person that it is great that he believes in certain ideas, but might it not be more effective if he wrote a letter to the editor of his local newspaper, say, once a month, stating his beliefs? Now, writing a letter to the editor is not a radical act. Because it's a low-risk activity, this person is likely to go along with such a suggestion.

Let us call this person Mr. Smith. We stay in contact with Mr. Smith to see how he's doing in his letter writing. We send him information and fact sheets to make his task easier. Eventually, writing letters to the editor becomes a routine part of his life. We then go to him and say, "Writing letters to the editor is great, but what about trying a column for your newspaper? It wouldn't take any more time, but in the minds of the people who read the paper, a column would lend more credibility to what you say. Why don't you suggest this to the editor?"

Smith, as a columnist, then becomes someone we might be able to get on media talk shows and to speak to organizations. He is now a full-fledged activist, recognized as a conservative leader and a spokesman in his community.

Had we approached Mr. Smith at the start with the suggestion that he become a newspaper columnist, go on talk shows, and become a prominent conservative spokesman for his region, he would have thought we were crazy. People become activists in incremental steps.

Similarly, if someone is needed to organize a demonstration, do not begin by asking him to picket town hall in front of all his neighbors. Build to that slowly.

4) The conservative movement has training programs in place, but they are not held often enough, nor are they within easy access of most of the public. Training manuals are few and hard to acquire. Most conservative activists learn by emulating the tactics of the left. This must be rectified.

5) We must also recognize the crucial need of most conservative activists for information, brochures, flyers, posters, and other supplies. Not all activists have the time, expertise, or money to design and manufacture all the material they need. Well-motivated, trained activists can provide skill, energy, and determination on their own. But often they have few physical resources. Give them the tools, and they will finish the job.

CONNIE HECKMAN: It is only recently that conservatives have begun paying some attention to state-level politics. The fact that Republicans were gerrymandered out of about 15 or 20 House seats in the 1984 election has caused conservatives to wake up, take a look at what is happening in the states, and realize that state politics is vital for advancing the conservative agenda in this country.

A clear illustration of the point can be found in what happened to us in 1984. Republicans received half a million more votes than their Democratic opponents in contested House races, yet won 31 fewer seats. In California, Republican candidates for Congress received 60 percent of the popular vote, yet won only 18 of California's 45 congressional seats because of the way the lines were drawn after the last election.

This is the message that the American Legislative Exchange Council, the group that I manage, and the over 2,000 state legislators who are members of ALEC, are attempting to drum into the minds of conservatives: state politics is crucial.

Some broad issues that are treated at the state level and are part of the conservative agenda include free enterprise, education, social welfare, the judicial system, constitutional rights, and fiscal responsibility. We have had state legislatures vote on such questions as South African sanctions and the nuclear freeze.

U.S. state legislatures have the power to tax corporations, license their operations, set wages, set standards for products and services, and provide opportunities for small businesses and minorities. Sixty percent of state budgets are devoted to education. Conservatives spend so much time in Washington worrying about abolishing the federal Department of Education. Granted, it would send a great signal if we could accomplish this, but it is the states that control teacher certification, student competency testing, curriculum, textbook selection, facility standards, wages, and a myriad of issues that affect what happens to you and your children.

Social welfare issues—the whole range of Aid to Families with Dependent Children, the block grants, Medicaid, and child welfare services—are state issues. Even if the states do not finance the programs, they administer them. We have tremendous latitude in some of these programs, particularly with block grants, to direct them in a way that is more efficient and more effective. Yet, despite the fact that billions of dollars are spent on these programs every year, conservatives spend a fraction of their time on the activities of the states.

Then there is the judicial system, in which there are three critical areas. First is the criminal area. The majority of the criminal statutes are enacted by the states. ALEC, at this moment, is in the process of drafting a model juvenile code for the states, because juvenile crime is on the rise. And there is a very clear relationship between juvenile crime and adult crime. Most criminal convictions are of repeat offenders. This is an issue that affects the daily life of almost everyone, which means it is an area conservatives need to be actively involved in.

There is also the civil justice area, and I put the liability insurance crisis in that category. The liability insurance crisis also affects everyone. The issue has been on the front pages of the newspapers and on every network news program. Well, 89 percent of the responsibility for that system rests with the states.

Then there are constitutional rights. There is "Baby Doe," the protection of infants, living wills, the entire question of euthanasia. All these are state issues. I would also put home education in the constitutional rights area. Approximately 14 percent of the states now allow for home schooling. This is an issue that is much in the limelight now at the state level, and it is an issue on which conservatives can make real progress, getting kids out from under the influence of the National Education Association. The

American people are not waiting for the U.S. Congress to decide on the issue. They are taking it up in their back yards. The right to bear arms is a state issue, and an important constitutional issue. The right to bear arms was not put into the Constitution to protect hunters. It was put there as a necessary safeguard from government coercion. If you do not believe me, ask this question: Would the Soviet Union treat its people the way it does if everyone had a gun?

The states have tremendous jurisdiction over the way in which elections are conducted, including campaign financing and redistricting. But conservatives spend all their time worrying about the Federal Elections Commission. Extraordinary!

It goes without saying that taxes are a state issue. I assume you all pay state taxes. If you don't, they will be collected. Remember the balanced budget amendment, which we cannot get moving on the federal level. Well, we are only two states short of mandating a constitutional convention to address the balanced budget amendment issue.

My organization has an annual budget of only $1.2 million, and a staff of 19. We cannot handle every issue or every state that is out there. We have only begun to chip away at the tip of the iceberg. State politics is not glamorous, which is why most ambitious people shy away from it. The news media place state issues in the second or third section, and thus send a signal that they really do not affect your life much. The fact is, what the President of the United States tells Congress on any given day is not nearly as likely to affect your life as a bill before your state legislature.

State politics is not sexy. But many important battles are taking place there. People always ask me, we have a hard time dealing with 535 members of Congress at the federal level, how can we have any impact on 7,461 state legislators that meet on an irregular basis every year? My answer is that we do not have to take it on all at once. You can only eat an elephant one bit at a time. That is how we should approach state politics: with hard work, persistence, picking the right battles, and extreme patience. Remember, most state legislators have no staff. They are delighted to hear from Washington professionals. In Washington, we seem to have too much information. State legislators often work with almost no information. They can use our research and our guidance, and there can be enormous payoffs. It is an area that has been neglected by both sides, liberal and conservative. But state politics can be the next frontier where conservatives can establish a governing majority.

FRANK LAVIN: There is a tendency to view recent conservative victories as "proof" of the ascendancy of the conservative viewpoint. Just as Marxists analyze everything on the basis of class motivations, some conservatives analyze events only on the basis of ideology, and ignore important non-ideological areas of politics. Voters look at leadership, effectiveness, honesty, and a host of other characteristics, and they sometimes ignore ideology altogether. Many people have a mix of conservative and liberal instincts.

Philosophy, or ideology, is a necessary basis for developing public policy, but its role in electoral politics is not central. It can be used, sometimes, to "smoke out" a liberal opponent who would prefer that his views remain hidden. But a campaign based on ideology will fail to reach broad sections of the electorate.

The key area in which conservatives are performing well is in waging the battle of ideas. Twenty years ago, conservatives were perceived as merely being against everything—racial progress, social justice, and peace. Now the Left is the defender of the status quo. This is particularly important, given the bias in the media and the public for activism and intellectual ferment.

The second big advantage enjoyed by young conservatives is that the Right has evolved into a "broad church." There is a great deal of interplay among the different conservative tendencies, be they libertarian, neoconservative, New Right, Old Right, classical liberal, or religious Right. The conservative movement, especially among the younger generation, is extremely tolerant of conflicting viewpoints. The tendency seems to be to find areas of agreement rather than of difference. As a result, there are the right-to-life people working with supply-siders, strategic defense advocates, and people waging wars of national liberation against communist rule. The conservative coalition has become broad, spanning a wide range of issues and interests and including people of all varieties of economic, educational, and ethnic backgrounds. No doubt this contributes to the ferment and electricity now evident in the conservative movement.

In addition, the Right has devised a plethora of institutional mechanisms and tactics, many of them, in fact, borrowed from the Left. There are conservative media outlets, foundations, PACs, legislative groups, grass-roots organizations, and policy institutions. Some of these are single-issue, and others cover the spectrum. The distinguishing feature of today's conservative movement is the high degree of interaction and coordination among its many diverse groups.

Chapter Nine

A CONSERVATIVE NEW DEAL

The New Deal coalition put together by Franklin Roosevelt and expanded by Lyndon Johnson has begun to splinter. Blue-collar workers, Catholics, and ethnic voters are leaving the Democratic Party in droves. The New Deal has become a bad deal for most Americans. The political challenge for conservatives is to address the concerns of this old liberal constituency and incorporate it into a coalition that has a concrete interest in taking power away from the state, while expanding free market capitalism.

MAC CAREY: There is not much question that we have a new generation of young people calling themselves conservatives, who are somehow different from earlier breeds. Maybe we should call ourselves "progressive conservatives." In the House of Representatives, we can see a model for how progressive conservative politics is conducted among the so-called Young Turks. Their conservatism is well thought out, but it is not just academic: They combine thought with action. They are intellectuals and people of ideas, but they put their ideas into legislation and apply them in election campaigns. They take their conservative proposals into the public arena and try to move public opinion in a conservative direction. Their aim is not just conservative, it is radical: to change the way business is done in Congress and in Washington, but to change it by moving it ever closer to the ideals of equality and freedom of opportunity envisioned by the Founding Fathers.

Something like this took place in the Democratic Party at the beginning of this century. After the Civil War and Reconstruction, the Democrats became known as the party of sectionalism and reaction. But after the turn of the century, a small group of Left-leaning intellectuals worked continuously to transform the dying party of the Old South into a broad-based progressive party. They had achieved only partial success when a former President of Princeton University, Woodrow Wilson, won the White House through a political fluke.

But their real success came after their ideas had penetrated public opinion, and they put together the New Deal coalition. The New Deal reached out to various disaffected groups, but the core of the coalition remained what Franklin D. Roosevelt called the "average man," the typical lower-middle income American family. Only recently has this almost forty-year-old coalition begun to dissolve, and the question is whether progressive conservatives can assemble a new coalition to make up a governing majority for decades to come.

To the Old Right generation of *National Review* conservatives have been added three or four new groups. First are the neoconservatives, mostly former liberals who have come to recognize that Soviet totalitarian aggression is the greatest threat in our time to human rights, democracy, and free expression to which, as liberals, they remain committed. Next are supply-siders, led by Jack Kemp, who have cut through the old conservative balanced budget dogma, or at any rate have seen that balanced budgets are a function of the dynamics of economic growth. The religious Right makes up a third group with its concern about the family and social issues. Fourth and more tentative, are blue-collar voters who realize that the Democratic Party's liberalism has rejected middle-income politics, but who also remain cool to the conservative movement on cultural grounds.

I hope and believe that there is room for a fifth group—the poor, especially blacks and other minority groups—whose real interest lies with opening up economic opportunity at every level. For those who are skeptical about this, remember that a majority of blacks voted for Herbert Hoover and the party of Lincoln in 1932. It took blacks and minorities years before they joined the New Deal Democrats, not wishing to give their support to the party of Dixie. Governor Thomas Kean of my state, New Jersey, pulled 60 percent of the black voters in 1984, and I think that when the results of the Reagan progressive conservative program become clear in the inner cities and poor rural areas, you will find sudden, massive shifts in minority votes.

What we are seeing is a new political mixture and an emerging political philosophy, related to, but not exactly the same as, what Barry Goldwater and *National Review* were preaching during the fifties and sixties. The New Deal, of course, was not precisely what Bob La Follette or the progressive intellectuals at the old *New Republic* had fought for either.

We are seeing a new populism that has not only been picked up by President Reagan but has become the immovable, if not yet dominant, force within the Republican Party. Republicans have become the party of FDR's "average man," while the Democrats have become the elitist party, reassuming their pre-progressive era posture. It is the Democrats who are the party of special interests, of academe, and of government bureaucrats, while the Republicans have become, or are becoming, the party of working and middle America, and even the poor.

The key players in the Young Turk movement in the House are GOP's Whip Trent Lott of Mississippi, Jack Kemp of New York, Vin Weber of Minnesota, Henry Hyde of Illinois, Connie Mack of Florida, Jim Courter and Dean Gallo of New Jersey, Newt Gingrich of Georgia, Bob Walker of Pennsylvania, and Dick Armey of Texas. There are others, and what is immediately obvious is that this is a truly national movement, eastern, southern, northern, and mid- and far-western. This national band of movers and shakers is remaking electoral politics.

The high-water mark for the Young Turk movement so far was the 1984 Republican Party platform, which contained three planks unambiguously calling for no tax increase. It contained severe criticism of the Federal Reserve Board and the International Monetary Fund. It called for considering a return to the gold standard. It supported tax cuts for the poor with further reduction of marginal rates. It called for civil rights and extending liberal democracy to areas of the globe where democracy is only a distant dream. The GOP platform, in my view, is a road map for where the Party and the Third Generation conservatives should be headed on issues in the future.

Moreover, for those who know the history of political conventions, the future leadership of the party often can be foretold by previous platforms. Ronald Reagan's nomination in 1980 could have been predicted by looking at the 1976 platform on which Gerald Ford ran. It was written by the Party's Reaganites. The 1984 platform marked the end —politically and intellectually—of the domination of the Republican Party by the old walruses. I am talking here mainly of the Republican leadership in the Senate who are, as ever, more concerned with balancing the budget than cutting tax rates, and who put the government's prosperity before general prosperity as if the latter were caused by the former instead of the other way around. The old walruses tried to keep the Young Turk planks out of the platform, but they lost on every point. They have since completely capitulated and have even jumped on the supply-side bandwagon.

Once Senator Packwood saw that his Christmas tree tax reform proposal of high rates and special breaks for favored businesses was going nowhere, and just as he realized he might lose his primary to a fundamentalist preacher, he came back with a proposal for a 27 percent top rate—more radical than the Administration's—and modeled on the Kemp-Kasten tax reform bill.

It is worth noting, too, that the people who fought the President's tax reduction proposal tooth and nail in 1981 and who continued to undermine it with tax increases through 1983—Jim Baker and Dick Darman—became the foremost proponents of tax reform at the Treasury in 1985 and 1986. George Bush, who called the President's tax cut ideas "voodoo economics" in 1980, also changed his mind. So we had Elliot Richardson and Gerald Ford-style Republicans out there selling our program, while the irreconcilables, mainly Dave Stockman, were reduced to selling advice to Wall Streeters and writing bitter books. Tax reform was developed and pushed in this country first by Young Turks in the House—Jack Kemp, Trent Lott, and their forces. The White House resisted at first (except for the oldest Young Turk in the business, Ronald Reagan), but the populist sentiment for tax reform proved irresistible.

The Young Turk economic agenda does not stop with tax reform. The next battle will be a re-declaration of the War on Poverty. Liberalism's War on Poverty failed. Poverty won—and the evidence is all around us in every inner city in this country. We need to use the tools of private enterprise to rebuild our urban sector: enterprise zones, magnet schools, education vouchers, tax cuts for the poor, sale of public housing to its residents at drastically cut prices.

These programs can be molded together to combat poverty in the U.S. But where the Great Society tried to fight some people's poverty by impoverishing others through redistribution, progressive conservatives believe the private sector is the key to enriching everyone. The Young Turks are now launching a political offensive on the last areas of the country that Walter Mondale carried—the inner cities. Progressive conservatism is already making headway in these areas because similar programs are working at the state level. They will also work as part of a national effort.

The Young Turks are trying to expand conservative ties to the labor movement—something previous conservative generations thought impossible. I call myself an AFL-CIO conservative. My two bosses—Jack Kemp and Jim Courter—are of the same mind. We believe in the goals of the Humphrey-Hawkins Full Employment Act. We really believe in something said by that dyed-in-the-wool conservative of many generations back, Calvin Coolidge, that there is a human right to be employed at a good wage.

We do not believe in using recession as a tool to fight inflation. We believe in the collective bargaining process. These are attitudes that we need to push into the forefront of the Republican Party if we are to be the governing majority in the 1980s and beyond.

The other major issue area for the Young Turks in the House is monetary reform. I do not know why the elitists persist in arguing as if money were some arcane subject only the technical priesthood is interested in. Monetary policy has been a major political issue time after time. Andrew Jackson's realignment included the issue of easy versus hard money; greenbacks were a major election issue of the 1860s, silver and gold in the Cleveland and McKinley elections, and the Federal Reserve under Wilson; interest rates were talked about in the Democratic platform of 1964. I think monetary policy could be the critical economic issue as we come to the end of the eighties.

The Federal Reserve Board has engineered two interest rate recessions in the 1980s. It deliberately slowed down the economy on many occasions throughout this Administration. But Ronald Reagan is now appointing members to the Fed's governing body who are promoting supply-side ideas that the Young Turks have been pushing since the seventies. Preston Martin, Martha Seger, Wayne Angell, and Manuel Johnson, the first four Reagan appointees, have already voted Paul Volcker down, forcing him to reduce the discount rate.

They contend that inflation is not caused by economic growth. They are warning about deflation. They believe that M-1 targets and monetarism should be abandoned. Martha Seger has been so bold as to say that the deficit is caused as much by the Fed as it is by fiscal policies. The progressive conservative revolution at the Fed is continuing. The impact, in just a few short years, of the populist, supply-side Republicans is remarkable. And I think it has only begun.

The most delicate part of the conservative coalition, though, is bringing together the religious Right with those primarily interested in economic reform. But I think it can be done, once you recognize that economic prosperity is not an end in itself. It needs to be completed by a prosperity of the whole person, a material and spiritual prosperity.

The integrity of the family unit is the religious Right's central concern. But families cannot thrive unless they can assure their sources of wealth and jobs. On the other hand, private sector capitalism cannot thrive without a certain kind of moral substructure. Unless entrepreneurs believe in the moral rightness and necessity of keeping their word when they make contracts, the free market will be destroyed. The source of the moral foundation for capitalism is the family, along with the schools and churches. As the founders of capitalism always said, those private institutions have to be encouraged by government for the private market to work. So I believe the social issues-religious rights conservatives and the supply-siders have a deep common interest in the success of progressive conservatism. George Gilder's *Wealth and Poverty* makes this exact point.

The greatest problem the Third Generation of conservatives faces is proper recognition of the real nature of the principles that have inspired Americans in their greatest times of the past—equality and freedom, human rights, and the natural right to self-government. The American people, to use Willmoore Kendall's famous expression, have always carried those beliefs "in their loins." The political struggle in America has always been a battle of ideas—and the victory always goes to the side that has translated the ideas all Americans hold into practical policy. I think the Third Generation does see that, and on that basis we are winning the battle and will govern into the next century.

PATRICK MCGUIGAN: The Third Generation has the opportunity to move past the initial political successes achieved during the last 30 years—and particularly within the last decade—to make ours the governing political coalition in America. We have to continue the development of an opportunity-oriented philosophy with adherence to traditional moral values.

Political success will also require that the conservative movement continue to be inclusive. One of the exciting developments of the last four years has been the willingness of the movement to encourage Democrats to switch parties and then put them in leadership roles. They have brought with them a perspective that has altered our strategic thinking, enabling us to learn how to reach out to minority, blue-collar, and other traditionally democratic constituencies without compromising our principles.

I believe that social justice and moral issues deserve greater stress within the broadly defined conservative movement. These issues have received condescending treatment from too many people in the Administration and in the conservative movement. On virtually every major tax and foreign policy battle, the moral issues groups have fought hard. Yet on things like abortion, school prayer, pornography, and more, the moral issues groups frequently have to fight alone. The most crucial task for the conservative movement in the next four years is to make the social justice activists full partners in what will be the governing coalition.

The outreach to new allies must continue. When people like Bill Lucas, who ran in Michigan for governor as a Republican and who is black, reject the Democratic Party because it has moved too far Left, there is a clear realignment potential. The same can be said of the switch of courthouse-level Democrats in Texas. The state GOP in Michigan has welcomed Lucas and supported his candidacy. This seems to be a good model to follow in other states.

GROVER NORQUIST: The Third Generation must make the conservative revolution permanent and propel it forward. When we make progress, we must make sure that we hold on to it and that we never put ourselves in a situation where we have to retreat. To do this, we need to learn how to pick our battles. Whenever we decide to go after a law, a regulation, or an agency, we must ask ourselves the following question: If we win this battle, how will it feed on itself and lead to future victories that will weaken the coalition that opposes individual liberty and strengthen those forces and ideas that favor freedom?

Conservatives can learn an important lesson from Mexico's dominant political party, called the Institutionalized Revolutionary Party, or the PRI. Before the PRI came to power, Mexico was racked continuously by revolutions with the government turning over every few months or so. But then someone decided to make the revolution permanent and created the PRI, which rules to this day. We need to do the same thing with the Reagan Revolution. I do not mean that we ought to imitate the Mexican government's corrupt and anti-democratic policies. I mean that we must do everything we can to institutionalize the conservative revolution and make it permanent in the minds of the people.

We must establish a Brezhnev Doctrine for conservative gains. The Brezhnev Doctrine states that once a country becomes communist it can never change. Conservatives must establish their own doctrine and declare their victories permanent, not only in foreign policy, but in domestic policy as well. A revolution is not successful unless it succeeds in preserving itself.

America's revolutionary leaders tried to make permanent the principles and ideals they fought for in a written Constitution, which established separation of powers, states' rights, executive veto, and judicial review of legislation to prevent government from encroaching on the rights of the individual. To a large extent, the framers succeeded in their mission, institutionalizing and making permanent their principles, embedding them in the fabric of American society.

In communist revolutions or coups the winners immediately move to institutionalize their position. Political opposition is liquidated. The leadership mobilizes the schools, the media, and the police so as to indoctrinate the next generation into becoming good Marxists. The communists always create institutions that support the party and destroy those that oppose it, such as the churches, the family, the free press, substituting for them an omnipotent state.

Ruling establishments in democratic societies also seek to perpetuate themselves, although in far less brutal fashion. It is in the nature of those in power to do so. President Franklin Roosevelt, for example, immediately went to work after his election. He took his coalition and made it permanent through legislation and brought more people into it. His legislation always served the political interests of the Democratic Party. Laws were passed, for instance, benefiting organized labor, making the unions larger and stronger. The interests of labor became one with those of the Democratic Party. Roosevelt created something that had not existed before: politically powerful labor unions that could be used to assist Democrats in their bids for public office.

Look at the teachers' unions today. Large, powerful teachers' organizations virtually unknown 20 years ago now lobby for public schools, an education department, and higher taxes. They dispense politically motivated propaganda for their Leftist agenda to our children. The NEA (National Education Association) is a critical building block of the liberal coalition.

Conservatives must discover the building blocks of their own coalition and thereby blend conservative interests with the interests of those who champion a free society. We need to increase our building blocks and tear down those of the liberals.

When we focus on the federal budget, for example, we could support cutting food stamps by 10 percent, which would save a lot of money but not necessarily be advantageous to the conservative cause. I believe it would be better to kill the Legal Services Corporation. Budget savings would be less, but many full-time activists for the Leftist agenda would be eliminated.

First, we want to remove liberal personnel from the political process. Then we want to capture those positions of power and influence for conservatives. Stalin taught the importance of this principle. He was running the personnel department while Trotsky was fighting the White Army. When push came to shove for control of the Soviet Union, Stalin won. His people were in place and Trotsky's were not. Trotsky got an ice ax through his skull, while Stalin became the head of the Soviet Union. He understood that personnel is policy. With this principle in mind, conservatives must do all they can to make sure that they get jobs in Washington.

Often we change from job to job in politics. We therefore should try to replace ourselves with other conservatives when we leave a position. This will ensure that, in our wake, others will continue to move the conservative agenda forward in their respective fields.

While personnel is absolutely critical to the success of any revolution, it is also necessary to develop policies that institutionalize conservative gains by bringing new people into the conservative fold, even if some of those people are with us on only one issue.

Take deregulation. When I worked for the National Taxpayers Union, I was greatly surprised to find that I was part of a coalition to deregulate the airline industry that included such liberals as Senator Ted Kennedy and Ralph Nader. They had their own motives for getting involved in the issue. Sears, Roebuck, for example, was interested in trucking deregulation, as was Senator Kennedy because of his personal hatred of the Teamsters Union.

It is interesting to observe how many on the Left are jumping on the deregulation bandwagon, even though it will cause people like Senator Kennedy to lose much of their political clout. Labor unions, for instance, will be pushed out of industries if non-union companies take over traditionally union-dominated businesses or industries. In the absence of closed shop rules, most people will not join unions. Non-union truck drivers will drive their own trucks and keep their profits.

In an era of deregulation, liberals, their supporters, and their institutions will be opposed by individuals who own their own businesses and drive their own trucks and taxis. These people, who are not beholden to liberal programs for their livelihoods, are going to be on our side. The campaign for deregulation, the effects of which will not be seen for many years, is setting in motion a process that will undermine and undercut the institutions that support liberalism, big government, and more regulation. Once deregulation reaches the point where enough people have a vested interest in moving it forward, it will become unstoppable.

Marxists have long asserted that they were the future and that communism is inevitable. Lenin thought it was his job to give the inevitable a little help. Stalin carried this to brutal extremes. A lot of people bought into that idea. Westerners said that we were moving forward toward world socialism, that capitalism and communism would converge. The American Left worshipped at the altar of "big government" for decades.

We are now, however, beginning to replace the Marxist vision with our own theory of inevitability. For example, we are moving in the direction of deregulation. Trucking deregulation is going to come. It is just a question of when, and whether it is going to be done through the Interstate Commerce Commission or through Congress. I think we have really set things in motion for continued progress there.

One of the biggest helps we had in 1981 was the demoralization of the liberals after the big Reagan win and the takeover of the Senate. They began to believe that a tax cut was inevitable. As a result, they did not fight as hard, and they did not fight as well. We created the impression and the idea that where we were going was where the world was going.

As we work to advance our efforts and make our progress permanent, we should look at some successful past battles and learn from them.

Among the successful local tax revolts were Proposition 13 in California and Proposition 2 1/2 in Massachusetts. Proposition 13 was a constitutional amendment, which makes it difficult to reverse or overturn. Proposition 2 1/2 is only a law, but because there is so much support behind it, it is protected. There were efforts to defeat it, but the opposition was beaten back. And because it has now been law for a number of years and so many people have benefited from it, it has the force of a constitutional amendment. Just as the liberals have always treated their gains as if they were permanent, simply through self-assertion, we need to treat our gains as permanent.

When the Supreme Court rules in favor of the liberal agenda, the Left immediately announces that tablets have been handed down from God and that is the law of the land. When the Supreme Court rules against the liberal agenda, the Left immediately goes to Congress and says this has got to be changed. Our gains are not, in their eyes, permanent.

We must treat our victories as if they were carved in stone, as irreversible. Only then will we begin to undermine the opposition's belief in its forward momentum. The morale of those on the Left will falter, and they will not organize as well or fight as hard against us.

The Reagan Administration's most damaging retreats have called into question the inevitability of the conservative advance. Had the Reagan Administration called the

1981 tax cut permanent; had it said there will never again be a tax increase; had it said all attempts to impose a tax increase by Congress will be vetoed, I honestly believe that we could have made it stick, and then focused all our efforts on cutting spending. By allowing the 1982 tax increase, the gas tax, and other excise tax boosts, our gains became negotiable. The enthusiasm of the opposition was rekindled. We must take the position that what is ours is ours, and what is theirs is negotiable.

We killed the Comprehensive Employment and Training Act, the most wasteful and expensive public works project of all time. But we gave away that victory in 1982 by saying, yes, the government can create jobs and we are going to have this gas tax bill that will fund these government jobs. We had won that idea, in addition to institutionalizing a tax cut victory, and then we surrendered it.

We have to continue to stress that cutting taxes is the best and only way to create jobs and economic growth and make that a permanent part of the American discourse. We have to present this idea repeatedly to the American people. The Democrats were able to take a fiction, which is that FDR [President Franklin D. Roosevelt], through making the government bigger and more powerful and spending money, got us out of the Depression. They have made this part of American history and something that is accepted as true by most people. Just as they have made their mythology accepted dogma, so should conservatives repeat their case over and over again: that tax cuts and freeing capital for investment and savings are the engines that create jobs. Indeed, the last four years have proved this to be true, as the tax cuts started the long period of economic expansion that has now created some ten million new jobs, more than even the most ambitious government program could ever hope to accomplish.

As we look for legislation that will make the revolution

permanent and lead to other victories, we also should consider enterprise zones. If passed, enterprise zones would create their own political constituency and a constituency for further growth.

If enterprise zones work, every city will want them. Mayors will be lining up on Capitol Hill to get their cities designated as enterprise zones. And because city mayors tend to be liberal, a major liberal lobby will be taken away from the Democratic side, as the political self-interest of the mayors will eventually transcend party allegiance once they see that economic prosperity is the best way for them to secure their political futures.

Thus, enterprise zones and deregulation are vehicles that can erode and eventually destroy large chunks of the liberal coalition. Once the liberal coalition begins to fall apart, and fall apart exponentially as time goes on, like Humpty Dumpty, it will be increasingly difficult to put back together again. As the liberals' coalitions splinter apart and become part of our coalition for opportunity, prosperity, and individual liberty, this maxim becomes even more true.

Conservatives have an advantage when making changes permanent. We are working with market forces. The free market figures ways around regulations, taxes, and assorted roadblocks. If conservatives can stop the liberals from enacting their ever-increasing list of laws and regulations intended to impede the free market, business will be able to make an end run, which is, in fact, what is happening now.

Privatization, which moves programs and jobs from the public sector into private hands, changes the economic incentives that the individuals involved face. Many liberals support public institutions because their livelihoods depend on the public sector. Change the economic equation, teach them they can make more money in the private sector, and they will change their political allegiance. Statists will become anti-statists—unless they are doctrinaire socialists, which very few people are these days.

The private school issue is key. Every student that moves from the public schools into private schools creates one less parent who is willing to vote for those bond referendums to raise money for government-run schools.

The more children in private schools, the more teachers private schools will be able to hire, and this will lessen the demand for teachers in the public schools. If we could pass a voucher or tuition tax credit initiative, I think we would see a hemorrhaging from the public schools.

About 12 percent of American children attend private schools today. Two thousand new private schools start up every year. At a certain point we are going to put together a coalition of parents who have their kids in private schools, single people, and retired people, and the liberals are just never going to be able to convince people to accept tax increases by saying it is for the children, when in fact it is for fatter salaries for members of the National Education Association. These are just a few of the ways we can help institutionalize our way of thinking and attack existing institutions.

We must always focus on how to take one of the Left's voters and make him one of our voters. We do this by showing him that his interests lie with the market and not with government, with expanding enterprise zones to the federal level, with allowing inner-city children to choose their schools by implementing a voucher system, with deregulating industries so that everyone can drive a truck or a cab or buy an airline ticket because he can now afford it. As these things become obvious to people, they are going to want more of them.

One reason liberals have been so successful politically is that they have identifiable beneficiaries. The Social Security system has identifiable beneficiaries, and they are politically active. Many vote only on that issue. We have to create our own identifiable class of beneficiaries. Individual Retirement Accounts do this. Vouchers do this.

This is why I am for countering liberalism's targeted programs with targeted tax cuts. Conservatives balk at this notion because they know it is more efficient and more fair to have across-the-board cuts. But if we target tax cuts, we can give certain groups more than others. This creates a very potent and powerful political lobby for, say, enterprise zones, or tuition tax credits. It creates an identifiable constituency of people who stand to lose something concrete if liberalism has its way again. Once we have our targeted tax cuts, we can then expand the tax cuts to include more people. We can cut top rates, but also get special tax breaks for certain segments.

I would support a flat tax of 20 percent, but then I would also lobby for every tax break imaginable, thus arriving at a kind of Swiss cheese flat tax plan. I would then work for a flat tax of 15 percent and also go for all the tax breaks all over again. This might sound Machiavellian, but it is also principled. If the objective is to defund government, then taxes should be cut, which means getting tax breaks for people whenever politically possible. We should be using the tax code, not only to spur economic growth, but also to put together the political building blocks that will form the conservative coalition of the future.

This should be done in concert with defunding the Left, which is largely financed through targeted government programs, and special regulations that block entrance into markets. The National Organization for Women receives government money, and so does Jesse Jackson's Operation Push, which seeks to register voters, liberal black voters, of course, not conservative black voters.

These organizations do not cost the taxpayer much, but these groups get enough from the government to pay for full-time liberal activists who spend their entire day, every day, lobbying for more government spending and higher taxes. Let us get rid of them. Let us get rid of the Legal Services Corporation and the special privileges afforded labor unions in the law, privileges instituted by Democrats because they knew there was a political payoff in doing so.

At first the cries of anguish will be heard. *The New York Times* will carry these complaints on page one for a day. But then these activists will disappear into the economy. Suddenly, it will be quiet. The press releases and demonstrations will stop, and there will be no more mass mobilizations because the liberals will have no more of the taxpayers' money to pay for their activities.

It takes only a handful of committed activists to cause all sorts of trouble. But if they lose their money, they will disappear. This is how to destroy their institutions. It is what liberals have done to conservatives for 50 years.

Let us learn something from them.

Chapter Ten

THE AMERICAN CAMPUS IN EXILE

The college campus has set itself up as a fortress of sixties-style Leftism at war with the rest of America. The rioters and flag burners of the 1960s have become the deans and tenured faculty of the 1980s who actually encourage campus unrest. As the nation in the eighties has moved Right, the academic establishment has lurched sharply in the other direction, and is now a captive of the organized Left. The greatest challenge for conservatives will be to regain a foothold inside the halls of higher learning.

LES CSORBA: Conservatives will not achieve victory until they capture the college campus, which now remains in the firm grip of the radical Left. If anything, the campuses are even worse today than they were in the seventies, or even the sixties, because, as the rest of the country has moved Right, the Left has retreated to the college campus.

Since the election of Ronald Reagan, the Left on campus has gone into a panic, adopting a kind of bunker mentality, and is now persecuting conservative students. We saw what happened recently to young Wayne Dick, a student at Yale University, when he distributed a flyer parodying Yale's fifth annual Gay and Lesbian Awareness Days (GLAD).

There was nothing obscene or crude in his flyer, certainly nothing as obscene as the films that were shown during the GLAD Week festival. But he was put on two years probation, jeopardizing his chances of getting into a top law school. Now, Yale has clear protections for freedom of expression in its handbook on university regulations. But, as Yale Associate Dean Patricia Pierce put it, these protections do not extend to "worthless speech."

So who decides what worthless speech is at Yale? Yale University's Executive Committee, in Kafkaesque fashion, meets in secret and does not issue written opinions explaining the basis of its decisions. Yale Dean Patricia Pierce delivered a verdict on May 12, 1986, that could affect the rest of Wayne Dick's life: "The Yale College Executive Committee . . . determined that Mr. Wayne C. Dick . . . '88 was guilty of a violation of the 'Undergraduate Regulations.' The Committee judged that 'BAD Week' [Dick's parody of Yale's GLAD Week] poster produced by Mr. Dick constituted an act of harassment and intimidation toward the gay and lesbian community." Keep in mind that the student was not found guilty of cheating, stealing, or assaulting anyone. He was found guilty of bad thoughts, which the liberals, in twisted fashion, called harassment and intimidation in order to justify the draconian nature of the punishment. As Dean Pierce put it, he was found guilty of "worthless speech," meaning speech that does not correspond precisely to the liberal world view. Gay and lesbian awareness is deadly serious stuff to liberals. There was absolutely nothing funny about Wayne Dick's parody to them. No appeal of a ruling by the Yale Executive Committee is permitted, unless the Yale Executive Committee itself grants it. George Orwell, call your office.

On May 16, 1986, Wayne Dick wrote a letter to Bartlett Giamatti, then President of Yale, and made his case. Dick said:

"I am writing to you in the hope that you will help me. I have just been sentenced to two years' probation by the Executive Committee. My crime was a satirical poster . . . which criticized GLAD week. . . .

"I have been told that my poster is not protected by [Yale's] freedom of expression regulations because it is worthless and offensive. I have seen many posters that I thought were worthless and offensive, but I respect others' right to express their views. . . .

"I most often express my views on the defensive since I still find myself in the conservative minority. To avoid heated arguments and to avoid hard feelings, I have often kept silent, even when I had strong moral objections to a point of view that was being stated. Recently, though, I decided to criticize an event which was . . . morally repugnant. My main reason for deciding to state my opinion more publicly was that only one opinion was being heard. I saw no real criticism of this issue. I am of the opinion that homosexuality is not an absolute good. . . ."

Horrors! Egads! Dick's letter continues:

"I ask that my sentence be overturned if the free expression regulation is in force or that the sentence be reduced because of my ignorance of the special status of the debate on homosexuality. . . .

"If my sentence is not overturned, please advise me as to other views that I am also not allowed to criticize, so that I won't unknowingly violate my probation and the standards of Yale University."

Dick's sentence was eventually overturned about a year later, but only after Giamatti was succeeded as President of Yale by the former Dean of Columbia University Law School and First Amendment specialist Benno Schmidt and only after enormous media pressure.

Liberals like to boast that it is they who are tolerant. But there is no free speech today on the major college campuses where professional radical groups are active in opposing U.S. foreign policy.

A Nicaraguan freedom fighter spokesman, Jorge Rosales, made a tour in 1986 of a number of northeastern campuses. At Harvard, he was hustled out of the hall as disrupters stormed the podium shouting "death, death, death to fascists." Rosales was hit with an egg in the eye and knocked to the ground by a herd of militants. At Wellesley College, Rosales was splattered with pig's blood. What a way to welcome a young man who is fighting a communist dictatorship in Nicaragua so he can enjoy the same freedoms we have in America.

But the campus Left is getting increasingly organized. As it has lost the political fight in the nation as a whole, it is desperately trying to hold what it can. It knows that if it loses the academy, there is no hope for the future of the Leftist agenda. The organized Left has been issuing warnings recently—in its publications—that its members will dedicate themselves to committing acts of civil disobedience and violence if the United States continues to intervene in Central America. More than 70,000 faculty members, college students, and associated members of the academic community have signed the so-called pledge of resistance, promising, among other things, the illegal physical occupation of federal facilities.

Dr. Herbert Aptheker, chief theoretician of the Communist Party USA, and now a professor of law at Berkeley, declared at a Marxist scholars conference that: "We have to develop a mass movement in opposition to intervention in Latin America and Nicaragua," urging participants to get involved in "imaginative civil disobedience, illegal action, mass action, . . . marching, sitting down, interfering with armed forces, interfering with maneuvers, doing everything possible." This is the kind of education the leaders of tomorrow are receiving in the American academy today.

At another Marxist scholars' conference that I attended at the University of Washington in the spring of 1986, I listened to a talk by a university professor on Afghanistan. His thesis was that "Afghanistan is better off" since the Soviet occupation of that country. He had high praise for the Soviets' paving of the streets of Kabul. Another academic added: "As communists, we know that the Soviet Union has the correct policies. This notion of oppression in the Soviet Union is nonsense. . . . The Soviet Union has never exported revolution."

And do not think that students are not influenced by what they hear in the classroom. Of eleven members of the communist politburo in Ethiopia, seven are products of our universities and colleges.

This is the political reality on the American campus today. The universities are living in a time warp. They have moved massively Left during the Reagan era and have exiled themselves from the rest of the United States.

Before we can claim a conservative governing majority, we need to begin challenging the Left-wing campus establishment aggressively. I do not mean that we should do this by using the fascist tactics of the Left. Unlike the Yale Executive Committee, I believe strongly in the First Amendment. That is why we began publishing *Campus Report.* Sunlight is the best disinfectant, wrote Justice Brandeis. Exposure of what is happening on the college campuses will bring market forces to bear on the problem. If we get the message out that Yale or Dartmouth or Wellesley or any other college is disciplining students for merely disagreeing with the liberal orthodoxy, then parents will begin sending their children elsewhere.

The Left knows this is true, which is why they have worked so hard to discredit my group, Accuracy in Academia. Our mission is merely to publish a newspaper and report on what actually takes place in the university classroom. The academic establishment has come back with the argument that the classroom is a closed forum. This is nonsense. Just as books are reviewed, so should lectures be reviewed. This is not a political proposition, just common sense. The Bible tells us that "any story sounds true until someone tells the other side."

So I think we are called to challenge the academic establishment, to let students know what to expect when they enter a classroom, and to provide the other side of the story.

I also think that more conservatives need to become academics. Conservatives tend to study diligently through college and graduate to careers in business, law, or medicine. Their priorities often center around their families and communities. They often do not want to become involved in nasty and sometimes bloody political battles. Liberals, meanwhile, like to perpetuate their careers in the academy —perhaps because they hate the outside world so much. They tend to grow increasingly bitter as tenured professors, contemptuous of the apparent success of the businessman, and resentful of the esteem he holds. Most academics view themselves as the most intelligent members of society and thus believe that they should be running things. They hate the fact that a grade B movie actor could ascend to the White House and become the most successful and popular President in modern times.

They continue to cling to their Marxist dreams. They believe their socialist utopia can be achieved somehow, sometime, by someone. If not Castro, then Ho Chi Minh. Ortega is their latest hope, but he is becoming an increasing embarrassment. This makes the campus Left even more bitter, as their socialist philosophy continues to be refuted daily by events.

But as silly as many of these foppish academics appear, we as members of the Third Generation, need to remind ourselves that the fate of civilization depends on the education of youth. What Wayne Dick went through at Yale is only the tip of the iceberg. Because the Left now understands that it cannot bring the majority of Americans around to its persuasion, it has resorted to fascist tactics. Upon a visit to the Northwestern University campus by Adolpho Calero, a leader of the Nicaraguan freedom fighters, Professor Barbara Foley screamed into an open microphone, and I quote: "He has no right to speak here tonight," and "He'll be lucky to get out of here alive."

That is what I mean by the fascist tactics of the Left on campus. It seeks to achieve its goals through intimidation rather than argument. It must become a priority of conservatives to begin exposing this behavior. The college campus has effectively shielded itself from any Reagan Revolution by instituting witch hunts to prevent conservatives from getting tenure, Orwellian trials to purge conservative students from the campus, and scare tactics to prevent conservative opinion from being heard. It is time to restore the principles of American constitutional democracy to the university. Then maybe we can begin again the discussion of how to educate the nation's youth.

Chapter Eleven

WHITHER LIBERALISM

THE LIBERAL-SOVIET ALLIANCE

On virtually every foreign policy question where U.S. and Soviet interests are at odds, the liberals side with Moscow. This has become an increasingly embarrassing political problem for them.

DINESH D'SOUZA: When we ask the question—as many conservatives have asked—"Does a liberal foreign policy and defense policy serve Soviet interests?" it is important to understand that in most cases we are not talking about motives. Rather, we are asking, "What is the effect of a liberal national security policy? Can it be measured and, if so, does it serve Soviet interests at the expense of American interests?" I think the answer to those questions is yes.

I think we should begin by defining the term "Soviet interests" because otherwise we could argue endlessly about what this means. Soviet interests are those which are important to the ruling elite in Moscow. We can determine Soviet interests by simply observing the policies, statements, and actions of the Soviet leadership. Let us take an example: Star Wars or strategic defense. It is not difficult to figure out what the Soviet interest is on this issue. The Soviets do not want the U.S. to build Star Wars. How do we know this? Reading the Soviet journals makes it all too clear.

Now let us look at what liberals want with regard to Star Wars. Liberals do not want the U.S. to build Star Wars either. Very complicated reasons are given, but regardless of what the reasons are, the fact is that liberalism advocates a policy with regard to Star Wars that is exactly the policy the Soviet Union wants us to adopt. Senator Kennedy and Gorbachev want the same thing, apparently with the same degree of passion. Yet Kennedy and other liberals say theirs is the most effective way to fight communism. Gorbachev has made it clear that it is in the Soviet interest for the U.S. not to build a missile defense. Since when do we oppose our enemies by doing what they want us to do?

Liberals and the Soviets are in harmony on many national security issues. In fact, on almost all the crucial ones there is a practical correspondence between the stated interests of the Soviet Union and the recommendations of liberals. Very often liberals and the Soviets will use the same rhetoric to argue for their positions.

The Soviets, for example, do not want the U.S. to build the MX missile. They do not want the B-1 bomber. They did not want the U.S. to deploy the Pershing and cruise missiles in Europe. They wanted the neutron bomb cancelled. They want the U.S. to make a no-first-use declaration for nuclear weapons. They wanted the U.S. to cut off aid to El Salvador. They do not want us funding the Angolan anti-communist resistance movement, UNITA. They want us to stop aid to the contras in Nicaragua. They are in favor of SALT II. They are gung-ho about the nuclear freeze and they hated Grenada. Sounds identical to liberal positions on these same issues.

Our philosophy and our values are diametrically opposed to the Soviet Union's on virtually every point. Our strategic interests diverge from theirs all around the globe. Our interests are not the same as theirs in Central America, Africa, Asia, or Europe. So when liberals advocate U.S. policy that coincides exactly with what the Soviets want for us, how can we conclude anything else but that liberals in America are serving the interests of the Soviet Union?

Indeed, even the Soviets recognize that their allies in America are the liberals. Here is an article from the January 31, 1984, edition of *The New York Times* about Soviet opposition to Reagan, which says: "Soviet commentaries in recent months have made it plain that the Kremlin would prefer either of the principal Democratic contenders—former Vice President Mondale or Senator John Glenn—in the White House. Their speeches calling for restraint in military spending and for a nuclear arms freeze have been very favorably reported here as have similar calls by other Democratic candidates."

This is Moscow speaking. Now, have you considered why the Soviets might prefer a liberal in the White House to a conservative? The answer is clear. Between 1974 and 1980, when we had a more liberal foreign policy, nine countries fell to the Soviet Union—Vietnam, Cambodia, Laos, South Yemen, Ethiopia, Angola, Mozambique, Afghanistan, and Grenada. Since 1980, when Reagan came into office, the Soviets have not gained a single inch of new territory. Indeed, they lost one country to the free world—Grenada. I think it is fair to say that when liberals have their way in foreign policy the Soviets gain a lot of ground. When liberalism stopped having its way, so did the Soviets.

Soviet enthusiasm for liberal candidates is also understandable when you consider the rhetoric of liberal foreign policy. In fact, it is almost indistinguishable from that of Soviet foreign policy. Take the following statement on Nicaragua, and I am quoting: "By what right does the U.S. try to change the system of a sovereign state using military, economic, and political pressure? In Washington, seemingly, someone has forgotten that gunboat diplomacy is outdated."

Try to guess who said that. Was it Walter Mondale, or was it Chris Dodd, or Gary Hart? Actually it was TASS, the Soviet news agency, on May 1, 1985.

The following is a commentary on the Boland Amendment, which prevents the U.S. from trying to overthrow the Cuban-installed government of Nicaragua. After praise for the Boland Amendment and warnings that the U.S. is violating it by funding the contras, we read, and again I quote: "Reagan is opening the way to U.S. involvement in a venture similar to the Vietnam War which has disgraced the U.S. . . . "

Who said this? Right, TASS again, June 13, 1985. But we could have found the same sentiment in a Mary McGrory column.

"Cuba is not totalitarian." Wrong. Not the Soviets. That was Gary Hart, a Democratic Party candidate for the presidency.

Recently there was a movie that was circulated and titled "America from Hitler to MX." Its brochure promises to expose America's top-level corporate and banking links with fascism. Now, this was not something handed out by the KGB, but by a respected liberal organization—the Union of Concerned Scientists.

"Ho Chi Minh is the George Washington of his country." That was George McGovern, senior statesman of the Democratic Party. "Dear Commandante, we want to commend you and the members of your government for taking steps to open up the political process in your country." No, this was not a memo coming from the Politburo, but an open letter from ten liberal congressional leaders to Daniel Ortega and the Sandinistas.

I am not commenting on motives here, but I am pointing

out that liberal foreign policy prescriptions and rhetoric promote Soviet interests about as well as can be done in the American political milieu.

You have to remember that most Americans do not like the Soviet Union, and so the liberal foreign policy would be counterproductive from the Soviet point of view if it parroted every Soviet line and was openly pro-Moscow. As a result, the liberals will make ritual denunciations of the Soviets. But what is ingenious is that many times, even when liberals attack the Soviets, they do it in a way that promotes Soviet interests. For example, the Democratic Senator from Connecticut Chris Dodd said: "I don't want people in this latitude to think about us in the same way that the Poles think about the Soviet Union." He was talking about the liberation of Grenada. He sounds as though he is deeply concerned about America's image. It would appear that he deplores events in Poland. Maybe so. But the effect of the argument is that it ties the hands of the U.S. and undercuts the case for liberating Grenada from Soviet-sponsored totalitarianism. And notice what a fallacious comparison it is. Unlike the Poles, who hate the Soviets, the Grenadians welcomed us. Recently, Grenada voted in free elections—a luxury denied the Poles—for a pro-Western candidate.

Now, Senator Dodd knows all this. So what is he up to? Spurious comparisons between the U.S. and the Soviets that try to prove a moral equivalence between the two countries and the two political systems are very common on the Left.

Here is Mondale, for example, and this was said by many others: "The American invasion of Grenada means we have no business criticizing the Soviets for their invasion of Afghanistan."

But the Soviets have killed one million Afghans since they invaded in 1979. Our troops were out of Grenada in a matter of months. If Mondale does not want to criticize the Soviet invasion of Afghanistan, he should tell us. Instead, he uses an equation of soft history, which has the effect of preventing the U.S. from intervening on behalf of democracy, and at the same time, muting criticism of the Soviet presence in Afghanistan. Obviously this serves Soviet interests very well.

One device the liberal foreign policy spokesmen use very well to advance Soviet positions and undercut American positions is to hold the two countries to different standards of conduct. I am not saying we should be like the Soviets. We have higher standards. But we should be judged according to the same standards, and liberalism does not do this. For example, the Soviets are permitted to invade other countries. This is systematically rationalized by liberals who say the Soviets are merely protecting their borders. The Soviets are also permitted to make alliances with anyone—alliances that are based solely on strategic necessity.

The U.S., by contrast, can never use force, even when the goal is to bring democracy and human rights to another country, as in Grenada. Also, American allies must satisfy a complex and escalating list of liberal moral demands. They must all be democratic (unless they are Marxist); they must all be racially integrated (unless they are Marxist); they must not have any human rights violations (unless they are Marxist); and, of course, they must forcibly redistribute wealth, property, and land—just like the Marxists.

Most pro-Western nations do not meet all of these demands. Many do not meet a Western standard of respect for human rights, though none are as bad as the Soviet Union or Cuba, much less Ethiopia or Mozambique. Because some of our allies have a less than admirable human rights record, this precludes them from being our allies, according to the liberal lexicon. By undermining our less than perfect allies, liberalism strengthens the Soviet strategic advantage.

Liberalism always accepts Soviet satellites as legitimate governments not to be overthrown, while it spends a great deal of time and energy undermining the strength and legitimacy of our allies. For example, in Central America, until very recently, liberals were for power sharing between the elected government of El Salvador and the Marxist rebels, but not for power sharing between the nonelected Sandinistas and the contras.

How do you explain this double standard? I cannot, and from what I have heard, the liberals cannot very well either. All I know is that such a double standard clearly serves Soviet interests by destabilizing our ally in El Salvador, while strengthening and consolidating the Soviet and Cuban-installed regime in Nicaragua.

If there is any doubt about where liberal foreign policy stands with regard to Soviet measures, the chart below provides a graphic picture. Compared are orthodox liberal positions on major recent defense and foreign policy issues with those of the Reagan Administration and those of the Gorbachev government. The orthodox liberal and Soviet prescriptions for U.S. foreign policy are identical on every major issue except one—aid to the freedom fighters in Afghanistan.

Reagan's foreign policy positions, by contrast, are diametrically opposed to those of the Kremlin on every major issue except aid to the Mozambique government and trade sanctions against the Soviets. Most of us attribute this philosophical divergence on Reagan's part to his receiving bad advice from his advisors.

But the liberal-Soviet correlation on foreign policy matters is stunning, virtually identical. As columnist Joseph Sobran has put it, 'Maybe the liberals don't have Soviet interests at heart. But if they did, how would they behave differently?"

Issue	Reagan	Liberal	Gorbachev
Pershing missile deployment	Yes	No	No
Cruise missile deployment	Yes	No	No
Neutron bomb	Yes	No	No
Aid to contras	Yes	No	No
Grenada intervention	Yes	No*	No
U.S. abiding by SALT II	No	Yes	Yes
Strategic Defense Initiative	Yes	No	No
Nuclear freeze	No	Yes	Yes
Aid to Angolan rebels	Yes	No	No
Aid to Marxist Mozambique	Yes	Yes	Yes
MX missile	Yes	No	No
B-1 bomber	Yes	No	No
Disinvestment in South Africa	No	Yes	Yes
Trade sanctions against Soviets	No	No	No
Sanctions against Nicaragua	Yes	No	No
Military aid to El Salvador	Yes	No	No
Aid to Afghan freedom fighters	Yes	Yes	No

*Many liberals changed their position to one of grudging support later on.

THE MCGOVERNIZATION OF THE LIBERAL ESTABLISHMENT

Contrary to popular opinion, Mondale was liberalism's best candidate in 1984 because he most accurately represents the condition of liberalism in the eighties. This is good news for conservatives.

RICHARD BROOKHISER: In political terms, the Democratic Party has boxed itself in pretty thoroughly. This is best illustrated by looking at the careers of George McGovern and Walter Mondale.

In 1948, George McGovern was a delegate to the Progressive Party convention of Henry Wallace. Now, neither Wallace nor McGovern were communists. But the Progressive Party was run by communists and stooges of communists. It attracted many non-communists, the kind of liberals who believed that U.S. foreign policy should be based on trust of Stalin. George McGovern was one of those people.

Walter Mondale, at this time, was in the youth wing of Americans for Democratic Action. He was a soldier of Hubert Humphrey, and he was involved in a project to throw Wallace supporters out of the Democratic Party in Minnesota. Hubert Humphrey, in fact, gave a speech declaring that, "We will not have a foreign policy controlled by the Kremlin." That sounds like a *Human Events* headline. That was Hubert Humphrey's Democratic Party, and Walter Mondale agreed with that back in 1948.

Now push "fast forward" to 1972. George McGovern is nominated, beating, among others, Hubert Humphrey. Fast forward again to 1984. McGovern makes another run, but he pulls out and announces that he would be happy with either Mondale or Hart. It did not make any difference to him who won—his former campaign manager or his former enemy—because the leading Democratic candidates now agreed on foreign policy and almost every other issue as well. So McGovern, though he lost to Mondale in 1984, had actually won in terms of shaping the agenda for the Democratic Party. He had moved everyone to the Left.

We can also see that the Democrats boxed themselves in politically, not because they nominated Mondale in 1984, but because he was their best choice. They could not find anyone better: Mondale expressed perfectly, more perfectly than anyone else, the essence of the Democratic Party. He was where it was in 1984, just as Hubert Humphrey was where it was in 1968. Mondale represented the status quo.

What was this essence? It was that the Democratic Party was the party of need. Mondale said this over and over. The role of government, he said, was to help people in need.

The problem, though, is that the number of people needing help with something is virtually endless. So he had to pick and choose. The result of Mondale's choices was a very tiny coalition, a minute alliance of special interests. Mondale would argue that he was not a tool of special interests, and he was absolutely correct. Gary Hart threw this charge at him in the Des Moines debate, and Mondale retorted: "Listen, these people are not supporting me because they run me. They are supporting me because they trust me." And they did, and they were right to trust him, because he agreed with them on everything. He had not made any deals. He had not sold himself for their support. Whenever they wanted something, they knew with certainty that he would go to bat for them. Naturally they supported him. It was clear-cut. And that turned out to be Mondale's "beef."

You remember Mondale asking Gary Hart that silly question: "Where's the beef?" But it turned out to be a serious one. It turned out that Hart did not have the beef, because he did not have the support of the special interests who control and vote in Democratic primaries. Mondale had captured that constituency. He had been working at it for a long time, and that is where the Democratic Party was. So Mondale got the nomination.

Remember John Glenn? John Glenn looked pretty good in 1983. He was ahead of both Mondale and Reagan in the polls. But then he fell apart suddenly and ingloriously.

Reporters did not understand what had happened to Glenn. They blamed it on Glenn's staff. True, his staff was ghastly, but that was not the problem. Glenn could have had a great staff and still would have lost. Other commentators said it was his speaking style. I have heard him speak. He is not bad. Not great, but not bad either. Glenn's problem was that he was not saying anything. There was nothing coherent in what he was saying. He did not give Democrats any concrete reasons why he was different from Walter Mondale, or why he was better. You cannot beat something with nothing, and Glenn was running with nothing. Mondale had the special interests, and Glenn had nothing. When the crunch came, Glenn faded very rapidly.

The only way the Democrats can get themselves out of the political box McGovern got them into back in 1972 is by trying something different. But they will have to find something different. They cannot make the same mistake Glenn did and substitute nothing for something. It is not enough either to claim to have new ideas, as Gary Hart did. He tried that and everyone said: "Oh, that's great Gary. What are they?" Well, he did not have any and he lost.

They might look at someone like New Jersey Senator Bill Bradley, who seems to be doing things differently. He learned about supply-side economics from Jeff Bell, whom he beat for the Senate in New Jersey back in 1978. Bradley switched his position on the contras. Democrats have already criticized him for practicing "me-tooism." And these Democrats are right about that. Bradley's me-too approach, of aping the Republican Party, is exactly what political parties that have fallen on hard times tend to do. That is what the Republican Party did through the 1940s and 1950s, and we know where that got us. The Democrats got all the credit. But now the Democrats are in that position.

It is really very difficult to know what the Democrats must do in order to get themselves out of this political box. I imagine that they will flounder through 1988 as their special interest constituency continues to shrink. It appears to me that they are in very deep trouble for the future.

Chapter Twelve

THE RADICAL CASE FOR FREEDOM

Libertarians and conservatives have often felt uncomfortable with one another. Ayn Rand was openly hostile to conservatives, and they to her. In 1969, an especially acrimonious split occurred within Young Americans for Freedom between the libertarians and the traditionalists. What follows are statements by two libertarians—Walter Olson and Doug Bandow, who wish to make their peace with conservatives—and a statement by one conservative, Benjamin Hart, who believes libertarians are largely correct in defining government's role. All three speakers agree that a radical reduction in the scope of government is called for and that the responsibilities of the public sector were clearly and specifically enumerated by America's Founders. Moreover, Bandow argues that any successful political movement needs a core of people whose role is to keep the philosophy pure, people who refuse to yield on their beliefs for the sake of political expediency.

BENJAMIN HART: The preamble to the U.S. Constitution spells out clearly the framers' view of the role of our federal government, which, paraphrased, is police protection, the common defense of the nation, the establishment of justice (the courts and judges), and finally the promotion of the general welfare of the country. The term "general welfare" in the minds of the framers had nothing to do with the modern welfare state. Liberals borrowed the term for their own purposes in order to sell various income redistribution schemes.

General welfare, as it is used in the Constitution, actually means the national interest or the good of the whole. The term refers to laws applied to the entire population equally. The meaning of the American Revolution was to create a government of laws, not of men. The state would be given specific and precisely enumerated powers. Citizens were not to serve the purposes of rulers; rather, government was to protect individual rights, which—as Thomas Jefferson says in the Declaration of Independence—are "inalienable." They are given to everyone by our Creator.

When we say that we live under a constitutional democracy, we mean that we elect our government officials, but that even though these officials are popularly elected, they cannot violate the terms of the agreement as spelled out in the Constitution, which is supposed to protect us from the very government that we elect. These terms say, in summary, that government's sole reason for being is to protect and enhance individual freedom. Thus the state has police power and the responsibility for providing for the national defense. Both are measures to protect us from those who might want to deprive us of life, liberty, or property. The Constitution also provides for an independent judiciary, which is responsible for reviewing legislation in order to make sure that our elected representatives are not violating the terms of the compact, i.e., their Constitution's charter. The courts are supposed to keep government out of areas where it does not belong.

Unless the Constitution specifically grants the government a particular power, government does not in fact have that power. Nowhere, for example, does it say that it is government's responsibility to redistribute wealth. In fact, that is strictly prohibited by the Fifth Amendment's "takings" clause, which states in unambiguous terms: "nor shall private property be taken for public use, without just compensation."

Thus, when government decides that it would serve the general welfare of Americans to run a highway through someone's house, it is required by law to pay the owner for his home and any inconvenience caused. So why then should government be permitted to confiscate property for other purposes "without just compensation"—for such things as price supports for farmers; low interest loans for corporations; student loans so people can go to Harvard; or Social Security for the elderly, who are the richest age group in the U.S.

All transfer payments of this kind should be ruled unconstitutional under the "takings" clause of the Fifth Amendment. Nowhere does the Constitution say that it is the federal government's responsibility to "wage war on poverty"—as desirable as this objective might sound to some people. What our Constitution does say is that no one shall be denied "equal protection of the laws." This would certainly seem to render racially based quotas, affirmative action, and the progressive income tax unconstitutional. Minimum wage laws are certainly a violation of the freedom to contract, in this case the freedom to contract between employer and employee.

Now, a government of laws, and not men, is essential to the preservation of liberty. This principle prevents our governors from using the power of the state to pursue their own interests—usually in the form of handouts to their constituents at the expense of everyone else. The framers were emphatic about preventing this from occurring. James Madison in Federalist 10 warned about "the factious spirit" that tends to pervade democratic governments, and about the danger of a "faction" or a coalition of special interests getting control of the government's purse strings. Surely the modern welfare state, through its system of wealth redistribution and racially based favoritism, violates any possible interpretation of the constitutional guarantee of "equal protection of the laws" for everyone.

Our Constitution guarantees equality under the law. It does not guarantee equality of result. But liberals, by using the coercive powers of the welfare state, are seeking equality of result. This is incompatible with the concept of freedom for the individual, which is that a person should be able to pursue his own interests and lead his life as he sees fit, exercising his particular talents and capabilities, provided he does not infringe upon the rights of others to do the same. Obviously the results will vary under this political arrangement, and obviously the framers knew this when they created our form of government. Liberals believe that people really don't know what is best for themselves. They believe that experts should be running people's lives for them—from some central location like Washington, D.C. Despite all its failures and all the misery it has caused people, both in the U.S. and in foreign countries, the dream of a socialist utopia lives on.

Liberals want a risk-free society, a society that is 100 percent safe. Hence, it takes about seven years for a prescription drug today to make it through the approval process at the Food and Drug Administration. The government wants to make sure all drugs have no bad side effects. Now this is generally a good idea, except when you consider the side effects of denying a terminally ill patient access to a partially tested drug. That side effect is death. Thus, many terminally ill patients, who need such drugs, are dying without them. Thousands of people are literally dying from public safety. Obviously there is a price to be paid for this obsession with public safety.

Liberals want society encased in a hermetically sealed bag. They want a neat and tidy society. But freedom is not neat and tidy. It is a bit risky. We cannot predict the future of a free society. We do not know what inventions will change our lives tomorrow. We do not know what entrepreneurial engineer working in his basement will come up with a formula that will allow the harnessing of fusion, or some other energy source that will create a limitless supply of pollution-free power. We do not know when someone will develop a fertilizer that will allow food to grow in the desert. But we can be fairly certain that government will have very little to do with the development of the really important breakthroughs upon which the progress of civilization depends, because most important breakthroughs are unforeseen, such as the discovery of penicillin, or the Wright brothers' first manned airplane flight. These kinds of things do not receive government grants. Government grants, by their very nature, go to established methods and procedures, which usually means they are out of date. They do not go to the genius who has an insight. Government subsidies go to sunset industries, such as the aging steel mill strangled by union labor—not sunrise industries, not a budding Silicon Valley, where real progress is taking place.

When Christopher Columbus discovered America, it was an accident. History is like that. It is extremely chancy. Columbus was not looking for a New World. He was trying to find a shortcut to the oldest of worlds—Asia—that would have made trade faster, cheaper, and more efficient. He wanted to get rich. His motive was profit.

Columbus's discovery of America was actually considered a failure by the authorities in Spain, and the great explorer died sick and in poverty. But other people thought differently. America to the next generation of sailors was a land of unparalleled riches and opportunity. Many trips were, in fact, funded by private investors. The first British settlement in Jamestown, Virginia, was owned by British merchants and settled by their employees as a trading post. Like many enterprises, Jamestown had its initial difficulties. In fact, the first settlement at Jamestown was completely wiped out by the Indians. But more British sailors arrived and re-established that small trading colony. It began to prosper, and soon they brought women and children and built new lives for themselves.

From that point on, the world witnessed the most rapid growth of civilization and industry it had ever seen. Soon Americans began building their own ships and began to beat the British at what they did best—overseas trade. The American ships were lighter and faster and could travel across the ocean in shorter time than the British Merchant Marine. The American sailors took more risks. Their ships were also flimsier and less safe than the British ships. But the American merchants thought the risks worth it, if it meant that they could beat their British competitors across the seas. The Americans wanted to make money, and there was no OSHA in Washington back then telling them their boats had to meet government specifications before they could engage in business. The result was that America got rich very fast and went on to create the most successful political and economic system known to man—one based completely on freedom, what George Gilder calls "the spirit of enterprise," a spirit that has moved people to sail across oceans, to tame the American frontier, to prosper. America's immigrants weren't seeking state paternalism. State paternalism is precisely what these early Americans were trying to escape.

Today, government at all levels consumes about 40 percent of the Gross National Product of the nation. This is dead weight on the back of enterprise. Can you imagine the kind of entrepreneurial energy that would be unleashed if we permitted, say, half the money now going to the public sector to stay in the private sector? Can you imagine the economic growth we would see, the opportunities that would open up for America's underclass?

In 1981, Ronald Reagan gave us a modest cut in tax rates and we saw the largest economic expansion in the postwar era: more than 10 million new jobs created in six years. Imagine the growth we would see if we cut top rates from the current 28 percent to say, 15 percent or 10 percent? We would have little to fear from the Soviets, as the size of the American economy would, in all likelihood, double every ten years.

This was the American idea. This was the idea Thomas Jefferson had when he wrote the Declaration of Independence. We were to be a government of laws, not men. That is how our government was set up. But this is not how it works under the liberal welfare state, which says that it is immoral, not compassionate, for a working individual to keep his earnings and dispose of them in any way he sees fit. If that is immoral, how much more unjustified is it for the welfare statist to confiscate money, which he did not earn, and use it for his own purposes?

In the minds of the framers, politics was nothing more than the perpetual struggle between the passions of those in power and the rights of the people. As Thomas Gordon put it in *Cato's Letters,* one of the most influential works of the period, "Whatever is good for the people is bad for the governors." The nature of power, wrote one 18th century American poet, is that "if at first it meets with no controls [it] creeps by degrees and quick subdues the whole."

Until the American Revolution, power had always emerged victorious over freedom. Individual liberty directly challenges the domain of authority. It is, therefore, not in government's interest to permit freedom to flourish. Moreover, restricting choice is what government is supposed to do. Government acts as umpire, regulator, jailer, warmaker, and sometimes executioner. Its function is to force people to do things for which they would not otherwise volunteer, such as pay taxes, or sit in an electric chair. The trick is to prevent government from compelling people to do these things illegitimately. The theory says that individuals have an inalienable right to life, liberty, and property, and that it is government's responsibility to protect these rights. But it is the very essence of government to take away all three. More importantly, it is in the interest of government to do so. Until the creation of the American Republic, no society had solved this dilemma. The framers managed to devise constitutional mechanisms to limit and defuse authority, thus making illegal uses of power on the part of the governors less likely, or at least less disastrous. Regular elections, separation of powers, checks and balances, executive veto, judicial review, states' rights, and open markets all served to protect citizens from government encroachment. And until recently, until about the time of the New Deal, our Constitution's framework worked very well. Liberal redistributionist politicians have found a way around our Constitution's protections largely by ignoring them.

Writing in the 19th Century, Alexis de Tocqueville predicted the eventual emergence of a new form of despotism in America, unique to democratic governing establishments, that would exert enormous and continuous pressure on our constitutional liberties. He described its likely character:

> [Over America's people will stand] an immense, protective power which is alone responsible for securing their enjoyment and watching over their fate. . . .
> It gladly works for their happiness but wants to be the sole

agent and judge of it. It provides for their security, foresees and supplies their necessities, facilitates their pleasures, manages their principal concerns, directs their industry, makes rules for their testaments, and divides their inheritances. . . .
Thus, it daily makes the exercise of free choice less useful and rarer, restricts the activity of free will within a narrower compass, and little by little robs each citizen of the proper use of his own faculties.

Americans today are threatened by just such a tyranny. Government has crept into almost every aspect of life, making decisions for individuals and consuming resources in a way not at all envisioned by the framers of our Constitution. Tocqueville warned of the great threat to liberty posed by an ever expanding paternalistic power that covers

the whole of social life with a network of petty, complicated rules that are both minute and uniform, through which even men of the greatest originality and the most vigorous temperament cannot force their heads above the crowd. It does not break men's will, but softens, bends and guides it; it seldom enjoins, but often inhibits action; it does not destroy anything, but prevents much from being born.

If left completely unchecked, authority will inevitably seize total power. In our constitutional democracy, this cannot happen easily. We will probably never see a military junta take over the Capitol in Washington. Government in America has increased its domain incrementally by paying off certain favored voter blocks through the federal trough with the ultimate aim of making as many people as possible dependent upon its generosity. This is how democratic governments achieve dominion over the population. They hand out taxpayer money and follow that money with a host of regulations restricting individual choice. Whenever we ask government to intervene on our behalf, we can expect a corresponding reduction in the area of freedom.

Tocqueville concludes that:

> It is therefore especially necessary in our own democratic age for the true friends of liberty and of human dignity to be on the alert to prevent the social power from lightly sacrificing the private rights of some individuals while carrying through its general designs. . . . No citizen is so insignificant that he can be trodden down without very dangerous results, and no private rights are of so little importance that they can safely be left subject to arbitrary decisions.

So said Tocqueville, and I cannot think of words more applicable to our present state of affairs. The U.S. today, with its bloated federal bureaucracy and budget of more than a trillion dollars, is far removed from the notion the American colonists had when they forged a new nation out of the wilderness, a nation "conceived in liberty."

As we look at the world around us, we can see that political freedom is extremely rare. Any student of American history knows that the road to the Philadelphia Constitutional Convention of 1787 was long and arduous. The creation of the American Republic came about under historical circumstances that probably can never be duplicated.

But Americans today seem reluctant to confront the reality of this conflict between the rights of the individual and the ceaseless claims of the state. Perhaps believing, after 200 years, that constitutional democracy is a permanent institution that cannot be torn asunder by the passion for power—or that officials in Washington are somehow different in nature from officials in other capitals—Americans have grown passive in their material comforts and seem largely unaware of the cost involved in preserving their unusual heritage. "The tree of liberty must be refreshed from time to time with the blood of patriots and tyrants," said Thomas Jefferson. He knew that freedom might be nothing more than a blip on the screen of human history, a parenthesis that will certainly close if we surrender to governors the power to make decisions that should be our own.

According to Machiavelli's maxim: "All human constitutions are subject to corruption and must perish, unless they are timely renewed by reducing them to their first principles." It is time to refresh our memories as to exactly how it is we came to be Americans and what is required if we are to remain Americans in the original sense of the word.

Liberty today is under attack in all quarters: in brutal fashion by totalitarian powers abroad and in mild form by proponents of omnipresent paternalistic government here at home. It should not surprise anyone that this perennial struggle between the rulers and the ruled continues unabated. As long as men must live together in society, past experience shows that this battle will never end. The Framers knew this when they established the federal government to perform a few very basic functions: the common defense of the nation, police protection, the establishment of justice, and the promotion of the general welfare of the people —and that is all. Any function beyond this on the part of our central government is a violation of the supreme law of the land and is therefore illegitimate.

WALTER OLSON: Let me recommend to you Whittaker Chambers' book *Witness,* which was partly responsible for converting me from a mere libertarian to a libertarian/conservative.

If I were going to explain why I am a liberal or why I am politically middle of the road, I would have to keep you here all night. Such ideologies with infinite numbers of contradictions take infinitely long to describe. It is very easy, by contrast, to describe what libertarians believe. We believe that it is wrong for people to initiate force against others. The only acceptable use of force is in retaliation against those who have used it themselves. All other political points of view, without exception, believe it is sometimes moral for some people to force, coerce, rob, or enslave others.

Everyone I know is libertarian in their private, everyday conduct. They do not commandeer other people's money at the point of a gun. They do not insist on breaking into people's homes when they are not wanted there. They do not restructure other people's businesses as they see fit. It would never occur to them to do most of these things, and if it did, they would recognize it as an immoral and criminal enterprise. Yet most of us accept the claim that government is entitled to do things that we all acknowledge individuals may not do. Libertarians insist on holding government to exactly the same moral standards that we all hold ourselves to as individuals.

If you or I were to decide that the family next door was not giving its child an adequate education and so took him into our custody or forced him to attend a distant school against his parents' will, we would as individuals consider this kidnapping. When government does it, it is called compulsory schooling. If you or I appropriated money by force, or by threat of imprisonment, we would call it robbery. Yet government does exactly that and calls it taxation.

If you or I were to force others to defend us against a band of marauders, no matter how just the cause, we would call it tyranny. But the government does this and calls it conscription.

If you or I print worthless paper money, we are arrested as counterfeiters. When the government does the same thing, it wraps the process in the mystique of monetizing the debt. For the government to print money to pay its expenses is sometimes faulted as bad economics, but it is rarely criticized as a moral failing—which it is.

Libertarians reject the idea that the government, or society if you will, is above the moral law. And they firmly reject the idea that government or society decides what this moral law is. They believe that the individual is the center of morality. They reject the idea that when an individual wins an election and becomes a government official or is appointed to a government post, he may act as if he were immune from that common moral law that bound him when he was in private life.

Libertarians believe that government has the right to do only one basic thing: defend us against assaults on our lives and property.

Libertarianism is based on the idea that individuals have rights that must be respected. Today, individual rights are rather out of favor in U.S. political discourse. The notion has been so thoroughly hijacked by the advocates of government intervention that it has become difficult to disentangle the true rights from the false. Liberals like to talk about the right to a job, the right to housing, the right to education, the right to adequate recreation, the right to attend community colleges at age 45, and thousands of other rights. These newly coined rights are different from and, in the end, incompatible with the rights the Founding Fathers had in mind when they set out the Bill of Rights. Those rights—to speech, freedom of religion, gun ownership—all fall into a pattern: They are rights not to be interfered with. Properly understood, there is a right to a job and a right to a home. The first is the right to work on whatever terms are acceptable to oneself and an employer, free from government intrusions such as minimum wage laws. The right to housing is the right to live in a house that you have bought or rented voluntarily from a legitimate owner, free from intrusions such as zoning laws that ban boarding houses. It is not a right to have a house given to you, but it is a right not to be interfered with if you wish to acquire one.

We have to choose between these two conceptions of rights. It is impossible to have both, and it is impossible to split the difference. When politicians assert that person A has the right to a job, they mean that some person B, whether a taxpayer or a factory owner, has an obligation to give it to him and thus has no right to keep and dispose of his own earnings as he sees fit. When politicians assert that person A has the right to get on a radio station under the equal time and fairness doctrines, they mean that person B, who owns the radio station, has no right to dispose of his broadcasting equipment, his air time, or his money as he sees fit.

The modern liberal notion of rights is thus completely incompatible with the libertarian notion of individual rights. The Founding Fathers took the libertarian side: They supported the protection of people's right to pursue happiness, not their right to be guaranteed happiness. After they spoke of the right to pursue happiness in the Declaration of Independence, their very next sentence was that "to secure these rights, governments are instituted among men, deriving their just powers from the consent of the governed."

There is an answer to the question so often asked of libertarians—what on earth do you want government to do if you don't want it to run the public schools, if you don't want it to file antitrust suits, and if you don't want it to determine which are sunset and which are sunrise industries? The answer is—we want government to secure the right of individuals to pursue happiness.

One of the most notable characteristics of modern governments is that the more illegitimate the responsibilities they take on, the less well they perform their proper responsibility, the securing of individual rights. Now that 90 percent of local governments' budgets are taken up with providing "human services," mayors and city councilmen have to devote 90 percent of their attention to the constant war among interest groups competing for public funds. As a result, the traditional responsibility of local government to protect us from street crime and other sorts of infringements on our property falls by the wayside.

The three functions of government that libertarians would like to keep are the police, the military, and the courts. The police to secure our rights against domestic aggressors, the military to secure our rights against foreign aggressors, and the courts to secure our rights against the misunderstandings, whether willful or accidental, that can cause property to be taken away in the context of contracts and other dealings.

We have forgotten that, if one of government's essential functions throughout history has been to wield a legal monopoly on the use of force, that monopoly must be strictly regulated. In a free society government may do only what is specifically permitted to it by the laws of its constitution, while individuals may do whatever is not strictly forbidden.

I would like to take a minute to describe what libertarianism is not. First, I am not aware of any religion that is incompatible with libertarianism. Second, within libertarian circles there is a tremendous range of views on the question of defense. Many libertarians adopt an isolationist policy based on the assessment that foreign powers are not really strong enough to threaten the security of the United States. I myself disagree with this, as well as with isolationism in principle. I think free societies have every reason, both in principle and in practice, to form defensive military alliances with other societies, including societies that are not as free, and that by doing so can promote their own security as well as do a good turn for their neighbors.

Third, libertarians have all sorts of views on abortion.

Fourth, they have equally divergent views on capital punishment. While they agree that it is proper to use force in retaliation, there is disagreement on the degree of force it might be prudent to use.

One other distinction I want to point out is that between libertarianism and libertinism. To use a flip formulation, libertines are the ones who want to buy dirty magazines and libertarians are the ones who do not think they should be thrown in jail for doing so.

There has been a notable strain of libertarian thinking through all three generations of the conservative movement in America. In many ways, the most sympathetic figure of the First Generation is Frank Meyer of *National Review* who spelled out what I think is the solution to the continuing feud between the more traditionalist conservatives and the libertarians. The word he coined for his philosophy was fusionism, that is, a philosophy fusing traditional conservative values with libertarian values. The term was, in my view, not that felicitous, because it implies compromise. I would argue that, in actuality, there is no real compromise or loss on either side inherent in Meyer's idea of fusionism. Libertarians need not sanction the idea of any kind of coercive action, while traditionalists need not countenance any departure from Judeo-Christian morality.

Traditionalists should be more aware that the government is a wild force. Many people would wish to use government as an instrument to mold character and to teach people to be virtuous—à la George Will, with his horrendous designation of "statecraft as soulcraft"—or to enforce traditional morality. But what one actually gets, after the laws are finally passed, sifted through the bureaucracy, their intent interpreted and misinterpreted by the judges, is a machine almost perfectly guaranteed to rip out and uproot traditional values.

There is a very real possibility that the next Democratic administration will move to cut off funds to hospitals that refuse to commit abortions. Likewise, the state of Nebraska is not trying to set up a state-sponsored religion; it is trying to regulate religious schools into the ground.

For their part, libertarians have much to gain in joining forces with conservatives. Libertarians have to acquire an historical sense and recognize that they are not the first people ever to have addressed the question of how government should function in a free society.

Libertarians should learn to shed their contempt for all existing institutions and acknowledge that it was Edmund Burke who remarked that he had never met anyone with whom he agreed more than Adam Smith. Burke was right when he pointed out that most existing voluntary institutions serve an important purpose.

Most important, libertarians and conservatives share a common opposition to the Left, an enemy that at home and abroad is at the opposite pole politically and philosophically from both libertarians and conservatives. Unless libertarians and conservatives, who split rather bitterly some fifteen years ago and have since been operating as more or less separate political entities, get back together, not to agree on all points but to resume the debate and begin learning from one another once again, I think that the liberals, faced with a divided opposition, will soon resume getting their way.

DOUG BANDOW: There is plenty of room within the conservative movement for radical ideas, which I think are essential for the building of any political movement. In fact, I speak from the point of view of a journalist who holds radical political ideas. One purpose of radical journalism is to build and reinforce one's cadres, the so-called hard core.

The publication *Libertarian Review,* which I wrote for, covered libertarian politics and internal struggles as well as general issues. It saw its mission as putting out the "correct line," on what the true libertarian position was on a particular issue. In doing so, it provided ammunition for the hard-core believers.

I consider such publications as *Conservative Digest* and *Human Events* similar, in that they speak primarily to hard-core conservatives, the believers. On the Left, *The Nation* serves this function, as standard-bearer for the hard-core Left. These publications are meant for the ideological shock troops.

Then there are the publications that print the kind of journalism that speaks to sympathizers, those who are not terribly outspoken, people in general agreement on some issues, but not necessarily on all. Regardless of whether or not conservatism and libertarianism are considered part of the same broad movement, we do not agree on all issues.

The magazine I edited, a libertarian journal called *Inquiry,* sought to be somewhat broad in scope. It offered readers commentary on all sorts of subjects—foreign policy, economic freedom, civil liberties. *Inquiry* wasn't as pure as, say, *Libertarian Review* in setting out a very clear, narrow libertarian line. But it did try to make the libertarian philosophy relevant to the real world. It tried to provide people who think about policy, whether politicians, or administrators of government agencies, or CEOs in the private sector, with ammunition they could use.

National Review and *The New Republic* fit this mold. Both are clearly partisan and ideological. They speak to their audiences. But they endeavor to broaden their appeal somewhat. *The New Republic,* for instance, even though in general it speaks to liberals and acts as an adjunct to the

Democratic Party, ran an article by Charles Murray critical of affirmative action. The message intended for the Democrats was that liberals need to do some rethinking on this issue—which does not necessarily mean they have to agree with Murray. Such articles will never appear in *The Nation* or *The Progressive,* hard-core publications whose job it is to propagate pure unadulterated liberal ideology.

Another kind of journalism needed for any healthy political movement, one that is intellectually vibrant, is idea promotion, wherein one tries to transmit ideas, sometimes radical ideas, to a far broader audience than the hard core of the ideological sympathizers. For a political movement to succeed, it must be able to convince people who view themselves as objective, people who are subject to changing their minds. Perhaps the best examples of this are the op-ed pages of newspapers. Read these sections in *The Washington Post, The New York Times,* or *The Wall Street Journal,* and you see that the editorials and columns each reflect an identifiable political point of view. All have large readerships encompassing a broad philosophical and political spectrum, and the respectability of the op-ed format enhances the credibility of the ideas presented. In an effort to demonstrate objectivity, these newspapers will run articles by people with perspectives opposite to the papers' editorial views.

Such magazines as *Harper's* and *The Atlantic Monthly* also serve this function. Both journals have a basic liberal ideology, but both endeavor to appear apolitical, in order to reach a wider audience.

Clearly liberals are far ahead of conservatives and libertarians in the area of journalism designed to have an impact on the culture. They have many more media outlets in which to publish. Consequently, liberal views are generally considered to be more respectable and mainstream, while our ideas, because they do not appear as often in the establishment press, are considered somewhat on the fringe. This is less true now that Ronald Reagan has been in office for a few years. Still, liberalism's underlying assumptions tend to permeate all levels of the culture because the Left has a much greater variety of publications in which it can publish and more writers promoting the liberal point of view.

I believe that there is enough talent in the Third Generation for a greater division of labor. Here in the audience is Martin Wooster, the Washington editor of *Harper's,* who calls himself a conservative libertarian. There is John Fund, deputy editorial features editor of *The Wall Street Journal.* Two decades ago, there simply were not enough conservatives and libertarians to fill those positions.

It is still vital to have cadre builders, writing for *Human Events* and *Conservative Digest,* to maintain the philosophical, ideological standard and to chastise wayward politicians for going off course. But now I think it is also possible to get some of our radical ideas about the role of government into the mainstream media, to make our assumptions become the basic assumptions held by most people, so that they begin to think of issues in our terms.

Building political movements is very important, as it is highly unlikely that the hard core will ever replace the ruling establishment. Radical writing and radical journalism are useful—but by themselves are not going to transform society nor cause a revolution in ideas. So we need to make an effort to go out and proselytize to add to the number of hard-core believers, and to get our ideas taken seriously by sympathizers and people who, though thoughtful, are not on our side. To do this, it is very important to get our views into the establishment communications media. When Dinesh D'Souza's or Greg Fossedal's articles appear on the op-ed pages of *The New York Times,* it means that their ideas —which ten years ago would have been too far outside the mainstream for New York literary or political circles—suddenly have to be taken seriously. A challenge to the prevailing liberal ethos is all the more effective if it is made in one of the liberals' prestige publications.

Infiltrating as many publications as possible—and I think we now have the troops to do it—will also enhance the importance of our cadre publications, such as *Human Events*. The thinkers, the people who follow the policy debate, will learn that in order to discover the ideas of the future, they will need to read our ideological magazines, newspapers, and newsletters. It is in the radical media (those that are philosophically pure) that the policy ideas are first developed and from where these ideas eventually percolate up into the mainstream debate.

Chapter Thirteen

SOME WORDS OF CAUTION

While an atmosphere of optimism about the decay of liberalism, the emergence of conservatism as the dominant philosophy of the eighties, and the future of the American republic permeates virtually every Third Generation meeting, two of our speakers were not as pleased with the state of affairs within the conservative movement or in the nation as a whole.

RICHARD VIGILANTE: The conservative movement—as a movement—is over. By conservative movement I am talking about the conservative movement as it existed before conservatives got into power, the movement that was spawned by the founding of *National Review* and the drive to draft Goldwater that, with a constant inflow of new recruits, worked for 20 years to pull off the Reagan Revolution.

When we hear someone say, "Is he one of us?" or "Is he a movement conservative?," we know what he is talking about: someone who worked for Reagan in 1976, slogging it out in the trenches, who supported Goldwater and worked for him, who worked for the conservative cause when it was losing, when it wasn't chic, someone whose formative political experience was the realization that it was better to lose and be right than to win and be wrong.

That old conservative movement was essentially a critical movement. It was not an attempt to govern. Its purpose was to destabilize the existing political establishment. It was an attempt to upset the people who adhered to the conventional liberal orthodoxy, who held liberal views because it was fashionable to do so. This was certainly true of the *National Review* crowd, which consisted mainly of intellectuals and journalists. But it was also true of the conservative movement's early political enterprises. For, up until the mid-1970s, conservatives always conducted politics in a prophetic voice. Truth was more important than victory. This was true of the Goldwater campaign. It was also true of most of the conservative activity immediately following. Some would say this was just the conservative movement being inept in its early phase, before it learned how to win. I don't think that is true.

People forget how radical conservatism seemed in those days. Conservatism in that era could not have been brought to power by even the subtlest political technicians. But that radicalism was, in my opinion, essential to building the movement. If we reflect on our own experiences, I think we will all recall that one of the things we found so exciting about being in the conservative movement was just how out of sync with mainstream politics we really were, how totally in rebellion. I think this feeling was one of the strongest forces in building the conservative movement.

A second essential and corollary characteristic of the old conservative movement was that it existed in an atmosphere of almost complete intellectual freedom. Because conservatives believed at that time that they were far from actually achieving political power, they could afford the most outrageous and unorthodox speculations about the political order. What did they have to lose?

Thus, Ronald Reagan repeatedly criticized Social Security, a very radical thing to do, which came back to haunt him later when he had the responsibility of governing. Some conservatives talked about monarchy; some wanted a return to the gold standard; some wanted to stop printing money altogether. Others likened abortion to the Holocaust, while others considered a 10 percent flat tax, based on the notion that even God is satisfied with a tithe. Conservatives took radical approaches on all fronts, almost as radical as a communist cell might have appeared in the 1920s. It was that spirit which separated conservatives from the mainstream of American politics.

It was by this very separation that conservatives gained their glorious intellectual freedom, which was a powerful recruiting device for the movement. It was intoxicating and liberating precisely because it was so anti-establishment. I know that for me, my introduction to Bill Buckley was a supremely liberating experience. Confronting cogent and often irrefutable arguments, for what were generally regarded as unacceptable opinions, taught me the most valuable intellectual lesson of my life: Establishment opinion is held in place, not by its compelling truth, but by the compulsion of interest and fashion. Knowing that, we could doubt everything the establishment told us—and doubting everything, we could learn a great deal. I think that most people had a similar experience after reading Bill Buckley. To see the establishment debunked was to gain a secret knowledge. It is one reason Buckley became a kind of American cult hero. But it was not cultism, because what we learned stretched our minds, rather than stifled them.

This freedom was given not only to the intellectuals, but also to the politicians. The famous Goldwater speech at the 1964 Republican Convention that everyone thought was such a disaster, in which he proclaimed that moderation in the pursuit of justice was no virtue, and extremism in the defense of liberty was no vice, was absolutely necessary. It was a call to arms, and it worked better than victory. For if by some fluke Goldwater had won the presidency, he would not have been effective. He would have been a general without an army. As it was, he never got to be general, but he recruited a tremendous army.

Commitment to principle, intellectual freedom, and radicalism was essential to forming the conservative movement. It helped recruit people, and it helped define what conservatism stood for. When conservatism began to attract single-issue people and interest groups, who were essentially offshoots of the central core, it meant that a body of beliefs was available to discipline single-issue activists. Thanks to the early conservative movement, the Moral Majority—despite its portrayal in the press—is not a nut group, or part of some fringe operation. If you listen to Jerry Falwell, you will find he is saying very sensible things that most people agree with, and I suppose that is what has the mainstream press in such a panic. The man is enormously sane.

Obviously, however, this old movement, this intellectually and politically liberated movement, had to end the moment we elected a president. Once it became that movement's responsibility to govern, its critical role was fatally compromised.

The day I realized this was around the time some movement conservatives tried to get Mel Bradford appointed Chairman of the National Endowment for the Humanities. It turned out that he could not become Chairman of the NEH because he had made a radical, if scholarly, criticism of Lincoln. He was not just opposed by the Left. He was opposed by a new entity: the conservative political establishment. In the old conservative movement, Bradford's freedom to say what he disliked about Lincoln would have been the paramount consideration. Indeed, in the old days, having a radically unacceptable view of Lincoln, or of any number of subjects, was taken as proof of one's intellectual vitality and noble disregard for the establishment.

But the new conservative political establishment could not afford such luxuries. Politicians must respect polite opinion. This does not mean that these people are not conservatives. Many of them are. It is just that this vast political army we have formed rightly sees its mission as taking the next hill, not making philosophical points.

Its job is to win. It is an army in the field. Armies are not self-justifying. They do not take historians and philosophers with them when they take the hill; they take the hill in response to principles and beliefs formed long before.

At the very best, today's political enterprise packages ideas. It will take an idea like cutting taxes and turn it into a jobs bill, as Jack Kemp did. That is about as good as the activist movement becomes, intellectually. It comes up with strategies to get around political obstacles. Privatization is an example of this—a strategy to cut government while keeping the potential opposition happy. It is ingenious. And it might work. But privatization is political strategy, not principle.

This brings me to my next point: Who is minding the store?

If the army is in the field, if it is winning battles, it does not have time for self-examination. Who, then, is providing that army with the philosophical and intellectual discipline that provides its ultimate motivation? Who is criticizing the conservative political enterprise when it commits an atrocity, as all armies do? My answer, at the risk of insulting someone, is that I do not think anyone is performing this function.

Most of the seminal conservative intellectuals, the intellectual founders of the movement, are dead, retired, or less active than they were. The younger intellectuals and journalists, those our age and slightly older, must understand that the conservative activist political enterprise is not something that they can really join in and become part of. What needs to emerge is a core group of conservative intellectuals and journalists who consciously separate themselves from the conservative political enterprise. It must be a group that, in fact, feels no loyalty to what is going on in the Washington conservative governing and political establishment. When the army goes wrong, this core group must be ready intellectually and emotionally to make as strong criticisms as are necessary.

It is fashionable for conservatives these days to sell out on South Africa. Conservative intellectuals and journalists have tended too often to say, "Well, these are our guys and South Africa is a politically dangerous issue. Let us pass it by so we can pick more opportune issues on which to take a stand." It is necessary to rebuke Jesse Helms for supporting tobacco subsidies and to criticize Ronald Reagan for avoiding the social issues.

The objection to this is that such criticism might destroy the political enterprise. But I think that such criticism would clearly define the conservative ideal in the mind of the voting public and would tend to strengthen the political and governing establishment. It is not our job as journalists and thinkers to let political lapses slide or to act as flacks for violations of conservative principle for the sake of achieving some short-term objective. It is our job to make principled and very firm criticism of these issues, so that when Ronald Reagan raises taxes, as he did in 1982, everyone will understand that his capitulation was not the conservative position. Obviously, this cannot be done by Citizens for Reagan or any number of conservative direct mail outfits whose contributors are loyal to Reagan no matter what he does.

We do not need conservative journalists who are partisans. Conservative journalists who act in a partisan manner ought to be rebuked, not only because they are dishonest, but also because it does not do the conservative cause any good. It is a waste of resources for conservative journalists to merely pat conservative politicians on the back.

The activists and the intellectuals, like the Apostles, are always bickering over who is most important. The intellectuals say, if we win the war of ideas, everything is ours. The activists respond that ideas without votes are worthless. Any sensible person must see that both groups are essential to victory. My point is simply that the same people cannot honestly do both jobs. If we do not form a core of conservative intellectuals with the same independence of mind as those who founded the movement, all proud talk of our having already won the war of ideas will come to an end.

TERRY TEACHOUT: America is a country in which the optimistic strain tends to dominate. Why should we expect anything else? Look at our history. Ours is a country without scars. No real domestic conflicts since the Civil War, no revolutions since George Washington, a long and cheerful history of uplift and success and doing the impossible. It is thus, I think, no coincidence that young conservatives have opted so strongly for supply-side economics, or that 60 percent of the American public believes that the Strategic Defense Initiative (SDI) will work. These are quintessentially American solutions, and America is the country of solutions.

This heritage of optimism has infected the conservative movement of late to a startling degree. The remarkable power of SDI as a right-wing rallying point is a good example. At the *National Review* 30th anniversary dinner on December 5, 1985, I heard Jack Kemp give a speech in which he made it very clear that a Kemp administration would deploy SDI as quickly as was humanly possible, upon which assertion a room full of seven hundred true believers promptly went wild. Greg Fossedal later told me that Kemp says that in every speech he makes; it is his strongest, most sure-fire applause line. Ronald Reagan is another symbol, perhaps the single most potent symbol, of the "new optimism." And the rise of policy as the overriding concern of the Right—at times to the exclusion of serious reflection on philosophy and our intellectual heritage—is the practical index of this optimism.

It strikes me that our generation of conservatives has turned to positivism. We assume that there is a policy solution to every problem; that human action can change human destiny; that intelligent, carefully packaged political appeals can galvanize the public at large; that man is a reasonable being who can be meaningfully appealed to through his mind. Those are exciting words. But they are also liberal words. They are at the very heart of the liberal ideal. The specific policies have changed, of course. But the ethos behind them has hardly changed at all—from Roosevelt to Eisenhower to Kennedy to Nixon—yes, even to Reagan. It is the ethos of rational man, of man the improvable. And it is this ethos that conservatives down through the ages have unanimously rejected as simple-minded and unrealistic.

Conservative pessimism in America did not start with Whittaker Chambers. It started with the framers. And it continues right on down to the Bicentennial. American conservatism, throughout most of its history, had been exactly the same as European conservatism in its essentially pessimistic assumptions about man's nature. We do not have to go back to the Holocaust or the Gulag to see that pessimism is the only possible response to the grim nature of the real world. The world around us is tragic beyond the reach of the most ingeniously tailored policies. Policy will not clear the city streets of the homeless. It will not empty the prisons of the evil empires of the world. Policy will not wash the yellow rain from the forests of Cambodia, or wash the hearts of men clean of original sin.

Do not misunderstand me. I know we cannot sell undiluted, authentic conservatism to the public-at-large if we hope to govern in the decades ahead. But to succeed, we must continue to remind ourselves that conservatism is much more than a simple checklist of road-tested policies. It is a philosophy, a coherent and consistent way of looking at the world. If we want to keep conservatism fresh and vital, we are going to have to criticize ourselves trenchantly, fearlessly, and ruthlessly. It just will not be enough to design intricate social experiments and express the illusory hopes of the American voter that there is a solution to every conceivable social problem.

Chapter Fourteen

A TRIBUTE TO BARRY GOLDWATER

Deroy Murdock delivered a moving tribute to Barry Goldwater at The Heritage Foundation's banquet on October 22, 1985, honoring the Senator from Arizona. Goldwater's 1964 presidential campaign trained a generation of activists and laid out themes that sixteen years later would carry a conservative into the White House. Deroy Murdock's remarks encapsulate the debt Third Generation conservatives owe to that quixotic but vital effort. Barry Goldwater knew that "ideas have consequences" and often repeated those famous words of Richard Weaver. But as Deroy Murdock puts it, he understood that "the consequences are greatest when those ideas are put into action."

DEROY MURDOCK: As I was anticipating this evening, I remembered the first time I saw Senator Barry Goldwater. I was a 17-year-old visiting Washington for the first time to witness a very special occasion: the inauguration of Ronald Reagan as President. A couple of days after the inaugural I went to Capitol Hill to see the Senate in action. You can imagine my naiveté. I expected to see, perhaps not 100, but at least 95 senators sitting at their desks pondering and debating America's affairs of state.

So I was quite disappointed to see that there were only

three senators on the floor. Senator John Stennis, the senior Democrat from Mississippi, was arguing for increased military spending. Republican Senator Strom Thurmond of South Carolina was there, and so was Arizona's Senator Goldwater, who sat at his desk with his hands folded as he listened to Senator Stennis's every word.

It occurred to me then that, as busy as Senator Goldwater was, he still took time out to show his support for a colleague from across the aisle who was as concerned as he was about U.S. defense. Barry Goldwater made sure that John Stennis did not stand alone on the Senate floor that afternoon.

As I pondered my first visit to Washington to share in Ronald Reagan's inaugural, I was struck by the fact that I might not have made that trip had it not been for Senator Goldwater's crusade for principle as he sought the presidency just one year after I was born. Barry Goldwater was guided by Richard Weaver's famous words: "ideas have consequences." But he understood that the consequences are greatest when those ideas are put into action. Barry Goldwater challenged America's thinking by showing that growing government at home and shrinking freedom abroad were not the only answers. There was an alternative to the status quo, based on philosophical principles and sound judgment stemming from reflection and, of course, common sense.

Though Senator Goldwater's initiative did not lead to victory in the narrowest sense in 1964, we conservatives did not lose. As I was learning to walk and talk in Los Angeles, conservative activists, thinkers, and financiers were busy organizing to hold high the mantle of conservatism and prepare for battle once again. When the battlefield shifted to California in 1976, conservatives were there, and they had found their candidate, and were successful four years later.

Through the seventies we built our strength in Congress and in the statehouses. The election of 1976 did not go as we wished, but it brought in the dark ages of Jimmy Carter, which went a long way toward discrediting the liberal mindset. Finally, in 1980, in the first campaign in which I fought, we conservatives were able to get one of our own in the White House. The point is, that in their hearts Americans knew Senator Goldwater was right; it just took them a while to do something about it.

As a member of the Third Generation of conservatives, I must express my gratitude to Senator Goldwater for setting us on the path that has brought us this far. Here we gather this evening, nearly 1,000 conservatives (and a few members of the media). We have not had to be scraped together from right-wing cells in the hinterland. We are the men and women who are opinion leaders and decision makers guiding the destiny of this nation. That is quite an achievement, and for this we must all say, "Thank you, Barry Goldwater."

But where do we go from here? If I can, for a moment, cite Greek mythology, our situation today reminds me of poor old Sisyphus. Punished by the gods, he had to push a huge rock to the top of a hill every day, only to see it roll back to the bottom. Sisyphus kept pushing that rock up the hill and it kept tumbling back down. This was to continue for eternity.

And for what must have seemed an eternity, we conservatives have fought liberalism, defeatism, isolationism, and pessimism with the same frustrating lack of results that plagued Sisyphus. But Senator Goldwater and the First Generation of conservatives were able to take the tumbling rock of the welfare state and international surrender and actually suggest that the rock need not always roll back down upon us. These men and women showed us that in fact we could defy gravity. By running against the odds,

Barry Goldwater proved to be the quintessential optimist against the defeatism of liberalism. He taught us that conservatives have faith in tomorrow, while liberals are busy defending yesterday.

The Second Generation of American conservatives, with the help of Ronald Reagan, has been able to push the rock back up the hill, thus stymying the disaster we have known as liberalism.

The rock now lies on the top of that hill in a state of instability. It is the task of the Third Generation, my generation of conservatives, to take that liberal, statist, big-taxing, big-spending, pessimistic, gloomy, dusty rock and push it down the other side of the hill and into the abyss where it belongs.

We must push hard to make Washington, D.C., a source of delight for tourists and not despair for taxpayers. We would love to put a couple of federal departments out of business.

And now that the forward march of communism across the globe has been halted, as Barry Goldwater a generation ago told us it must be, it is the goal of the Third Generation to push the rock of communism and Leninist tyranny down the hill and into the muck from which it erupted in 1917. We must push hard until eventually The Heritage Foundation and other conservative groups can open offices to advise governments in democratic Havana, democratic Budapest, democratic Prague, democratic Hanoi, democratic Phnom Penh, democratic Luanda, democratic Kabul, and democratic Managua.

It must also be the task of the Third Generation to challenge the basic assumptions of the American people on issues of public policy. I believe sincerely that for us to effect everlasting change in America we need to do much more than just tinker with the budget or pass piecemeal legislation, important as these activities are. If we are truly going to fulfill the legacy of Barry Goldwater and leave our stamp on this nation as he has, we will have to engineer paradigmatic shifts in U.S. thinking.

For instance, the posturing and antagonism between the U.S. and the USSR must seem puzzling to an American if he does not see any significant difference between the two nations. The U.S. defense buildup and our need ultimately to free people from the Soviet Empire will make sense only when the American public realizes that the Soviet Union is not morally equivalent to the United States but indeed is the moral equivalent of the Third Reich.

Shifting the paradigms that guide America's thinking is quite a task, but it seems to be the next logical step in the development of the American conservative movement.

Were it not for the courageous, selfless, and uncompromising work that Senator Goldwater has performed for years in advancing the beliefs that we all share, this world likely would have been an entirely different place. At home, some stifling form of socialism might exist. U.S. strength abroad might be much weaker, and the forces of communism might have captured even more victims.

As we young conservatives of the Third Generation prepare to guide the movement in which we are all involved, we find ourselves in a relatively strong position. We have inherited a far better nation than we would have just a few years ago, and we live in a world which, though often perilous, is filled with hope for the prospect of peace with freedom. Perhaps most important, our conservative philosophy is no longer seen as an embarrassing superstition, but now constitutes the articles of faith of our president with whom the majority of Americans agree. We have a long way to go, but we have already come a long way. And to a far greater extent than we can imagine, we have Senator Barry Goldwater to thank for that. Senator Goldwater, from the Third Generation, thank you very much.

THE PARTICIPANTS

DOUG BANDOW: Born in 1957, Doug Bandow is the most prolific writer and journalist of the Third Generation. He has authored literally hundreds of articles and has appeared in all the major newspapers, including *The New York Times, The Wall Street Journal, The Washington Post, The Los Angeles Times,* and *The Chicago Tribune.* He has also edited two books, both published by The Heritage Foundation: *U.S. Aid to the Developing World: A Free Market Agenda* (1985) and *Protecting the Environment: A Free Market Strategy* (1986).

Doug is currently a senior fellow at the Cato Institute in Washington and a nationally syndicated columnist with the Copley News Service. A contributing editor for *Reason* magazine, Doug has also been a visiting fellow at The Heritage Foundation.

From 1982 to 1984, Doug edited *Inquiry* magazine, a monthly journal of public policy and political affairs. Before that, he served in the White House as a special assistant to President Reagan for policy development. While at the White House, Doug was a deputy representative to the United Nations Conference on the Law of the Sea, which eventually blocked the Law of the Sea Treaty, a fortunate development according to those who care about the free market and world economic development. Also while at the White House, Doug served as deputy assistant director of the Office of Policy Development for Legal Affairs.

Upon leaving the White House, Doug published what may be his most famous article, "Power Can Be Fun," in *National Review,* an extremely amusing account in which he describes the President's close advisers as being more concerned with White House perks, what office they are assigned to, and whether they have good seats at important dinners, than with advancing the President's policies. "Perks rather than principles," seems to be the *modus operandi* over there, he muses.

Doug received a B.S. in economics from Florida State University in 1976 and a J.D. from Stanford Law School in 1979. A member of both the California and D.C. bars, Doug has chosen to pursue a career in journalism rather than a potentially lucrative law career.

On July 11, 1984, Doug spoke to the Third Generation on "The Role of Radical Ideas in the Third Generation."

JOHN BARNES: Born in 1960, John Barnes is chief editorial writer for *The Boston Herald.* A native of Brooklyn, New York, he took his bachelor's degree in journalism from New York University in 1982, during which time he worked as an intern at William F. Buckley's *National Review.* Immediately after graduation, he joined *The Washington Times* as a city reporter, covering Virginia and D.C. politics in addition to Capitol Hill and the White House. His reporting helped to expose wrongdoing in D.C.'s lottery board.

In March of 1984, John went to work for syndicated columnists Roland Evans and Robert Novak as a national political reporter. He covered the 1984 Republican National Convention and other events of the campaign, as well as federal and state tax policy for *The Evans and Novak Tax Report.* He joined *The Boston Herald* in May of 1986.

John has published articles in *The Wall Street Journal, Policy Review, The Detroit News, National Review, The American Spectator, The Political Report, The Washington Journalism Review, Election Politics, Human Events,* and other publications. Several of his articles have been entered into the *Congressional Record.*

On May 22, 1985, John spoke to the Third Generation on "How Opinion is Formed in Washington: Lessons for Third Generation Conservatives."

RICHARD BROOKHISER: Born in 1955, Rick Brookhiser published his first article in *National Review* at the age of 14. He became a conservative when he read *Up From Liberalism* by William F. Buckley. Rick's father had picked up a paperback copy of the book one day while in a drugstore. He had recognized Buckley as the host of the television talk show *Firing Line* and thought it would be interesting to read what he had to say. Before reading *Up From Liberalism,* the Brookhisers "watched *Firing Line* for entertainment, not politics."

While at Yale, Rick was chairman of the Party of the Right and wrote a political column for *The Yale Daily News.* Well-known as a conservative on campus, Rick once got into a paint-throwing melee with leftist students, who were writing graffiti celebrating the fall of Saigon. Meanwhile, he continued to write for *National Review,* and Buckley took him on as an intern between his junior and senior years.

After graduating Phi Beta Kappa from Yale, Rick was hired as an associate editor for *National Review* and within two years was promoted to senior editor. Upon the retirement of Priscilla Buckley, the managing editor of *National Review* for so many years, Rick assumed her title and duties in 1985.

Rick's articles have appeared in *The New York Times, The American Spectator,* and other publications. He is author of *The Outside Story* a book about the 1984 presidential election, which Terry Teachout, writing for *The American Spectator,* called "a witty and compelling argument for the good sense of the American people."

On July 11, 1986, Rick Brookhiser, widely considered an eventual successor to Buckley at *National Review,* spoke to the Third Generation on "Obstacles and Opportunities for Continuing the Conservative Revolution."

FRANK CANNON: Born in 1958, Frank Cannon is another member of what *The Washington Post* calls "the Dartmouth mafia." In 1979, he founded the Dartmouth Conservative Union, which, despite opposition from the administration, gained a student membership of 250. He also ran Students for Reagan at Dartmouth in 1980. Not a journalist, Frank is unusual for a Dartmouth conservative in that he never worked for *The Dartmouth Review.* He considers himself a "nuts and bolts" political operator.

At age 24, he was hired by Congressman Duncan Hunter of California to be his chief of staff, making Frank the youngest on Capitol Hill to hold that position. After two years, he went on to be the chief of staff for Texas freshman Congressman Mac Sweeney. He has since become the deputy director of Jack Kemp's political action committee, Campaign for Prosperity.

Frank takes pride in his Italian, Roman Catholic, blue-collar background. "I was under the median income for Dartmouth students," he says. "The rich ones were in the

Dartmouth Radical Union, not the Dartmouth Conservative Union." His father is a former labor union president on Long Island and his mother is a member of the International Ladies Garment Workers Union. He remembers that his family car once carried a Kennedy bumper sticker and says his family is representative of Democrats who have moved toward the Republican Party.

On January 17, 1984, Frank spoke to the Third Generation on "How the Third Generation Can Win on Capitol Hill," and again on October 29, 1986, on "Have We Seen a Conservative Revolution?"

MERRICK 'MAC' CAREY: Born in 1957, Mac Carey began his political career as research director for the first U.S. Senate campaign of Jeff Bell of New Jersey in 1978. Although Bell lost to Democrat Bill Bradley in that race, his victory over liberal Republican Clifford Case, using tax cuts as his major campaign theme, foreshadowed the nationwide tax revolt that would culminate in the election of Ronald Reagan. Mac also worked on Jeff Bell's second race for the Senate in 1982, and between campaigns he was executive assistant to the president of the Manhattan Institute in New York City.

Mac went on to become Jack Kemp's press secretary, a job he held for two years, until 1984, when he was hired by New Jersey Republican Congressman Jim Courter as his chief of staff. Since joining Courter, the New Jersey congressman, relatively unknown previously, has achieved a national reputation as the point man for conservatives in the House on such issues as military reform, arms control, the Strategic Defense Initiative, and terrorism. This change in Courter's approach has been credited in large part to Mac Carey's guidance.

Mac describes himself as a "progressive conservative," by which he means a conservative who identifies not with America's elite, but with "the average man earning an average salary." He believes strongly in tax cuts targeted toward the middle class as not only the best way to spur economic growth, but also as the best way to ensure that conservatives remain the dominant political force in America for decades to come.

On June 19, 1985, Mac spoke to the Third Generation about "The Young Turks in the House: How Progressive Conservatism is Reshaping American Politics."

LES CSORBA: Born in 1963, Les first achieved national attention when he was nearly expelled from the University of California at Davis for criticizing the lectures of Professor Saul Landau, which Les saw as biased, inaccurate, and excessively complimentary of the policies of Fidel Castro. Les was saved from expulsion when California State Senator H. L. Richardson intervened on his behalf. As an undergraduate, Les assisted in the founding of the *Davis Dossier,* a conservative student newspaper, and worked as a press aide to U.S. Senator Pete Wilson. In response to his reputation as a conservative student activist, the radical Left organized a demonstration at Les Csorba's graduation ceremonies, and he was roundly booed when awarded his diploma.

Les has since moved to Washington, D.C., to become executive director of Accuracy in Academia, which has received enormous attention in the national media. He is the founder and executive editor of *Campus Report,* which specializes in uncovering biased lectures and the persecution of students who do not subscribe to the political views of particular professors. He is the author of a monograph entitled *Appeasing the Censors,* published by Accuracy in Academia, which details the threat to free speech on the campuses.

Les has appeared on many radio and television talk shows, including news programs on all three television networks, as well as Cable News Network's *Daywatch* program. His articles have appeared in *USA Today, The Washington Times,* and *Human Events.* His family emigrated from Hungary, where his father fought against invading Soviet troops.

His talk to the Third Generation group, on August 20, 1986, was titled "The Campus in Exile from America."

DINESH D'SOUZA: Born in 1961, Dinesh D'Souza is the managing editor of *Policy Review* and a frequent contributor to *National Review* and *The American Spectator.* His articles have appeared in *The Washington Post, The New York Times, The Los Angeles Times, Harper's, Vanity Fair,* and other publications. He is the author of *Before the Millennium,* a biography of Jerry Falwell, and *The Catholic Classics.* One of the outstanding journalists of the Third Generation, Dinesh began his journalism career at *The Dartmouth Review.*

Originally from Bombay, India, he did not consider himself political when he first arrived on the Dartmouth campus. But then he received an invitation to a college-sponsored dance. When he arrived, he found that the men were dancing with the men and the women with the women. The dance had been organized by the Gay Student Alliance, which was funded by the college with student tuition money. Armed with an electric typewriter, it was not long before he began crusading in the pages of *The Dartmouth Review* for a return to moral and intellectual standards.

Dinesh spoke on two occasions to the Third Generation: on January 3, 1984, when he discussed "Why Conservatives

Have Failed to Present Their Case to the Media," and on July 24, 1985, when he debated Tip O'Neill's top aide, Christopher Matthews, on the question: "Does a Liberal Foreign Policy Serve Soviet Interests?"

PETER FERRARA: Born in 1954, Peter Ferrara is a graduate of Harvard University and Harvard Law School. From 1979 to 1981 he worked as an associate at the law firm of Cravath, Swaine and Moore in New York City. From 1981 to 1983, he served as a domestic policy official in the Reagan Administration, first in the Office of Policy Development at the Department of Housing and Urban Development and then at the White House Office of Policy Development.

While in the Reagan Administration, Peter served as a senior staff member of the Administration's Task Force on Enterprise Zones. He also worked on Social Security, welfare, and other human resource issues. He caused something of a political storm for the White House when he authored two books, both published by the Cato Institute in Washington, D.C.: *Social Security: The Inherent Contradiction* in 1981; and *Social Security: Averting the Crisis* in 1982.

In 1984, he served a one-year term as a presidential appointee to the board of directors of the Legal Services Corporation before leaving government to join the D.C. law firm of Shaw, Pittman, Potts and Trowbridge. His main hobby still is proposing private sector alternatives to Social Security, Medicare, and redistributive welfare schemes. His most recent book, *Social Security: Prospects for Reform,* also published by the Cato Institute, has received wide attention. Peter is also a contributing author of *Mandate for Leadership,* an agenda for national policy published in 1984 by The Heritage Foundation.

In his legal practice, Peter specializes in litigation, administrative law, and public policy counseling. He is a member of both the New York and D.C. bars.

On September 19, 1984, Peter spoke to the Third Generation on "How the Third Generation Can Cut the Federal Budget in Half and Still Win Elections."

GREGORY FOSSEDAL: Born in 1959, Greg Fossedal was described by *The Washington Post* as "the most promising journalist of his generation." He began his journalism career at Dartmouth College when he worked his way up from sports editor to editor-in-chief of *The Dartmouth,* the official student daily of the college. He was, however, ousted from the school paper by the board of directors for his conservative editorial views. He then teamed up with a group of campus conservatives to begin publishing a new newspaper, which they named *The Dartmouth Review.*

The *Review* is one of the first, the most outrageous, and certainly the best-known of the 75 conservative student newspapers that now dot campuses across the country. Greg went on to become an editorial writer for *The Washington Times, The San Diego Union,* and then *The Wall Street Journal.* In addition, he co-authored, with General Dan Graham, *A Defense that Defends* on the feasibility of a missile defense system. He has also moved from *The Wall Street Journal* to the Hoover Institution on War, Revolution and Peace at Stanford University, where he is the media fellow.

Greg writes a twice weekly column for Copley News Service. His articles have appeared in *The New York Times, Policy Review, The American Spectator, Harper's* magazine, and numerous other publications.

Greg earned some notoriety at the famous news conference held by vice presidential candidate Geraldine Ferraro to field questions about her non-compliance with congressional financial disclosure rules. Tired of Ferraro's evasions of every sticky question, Greg at one point yelled, "Answer it!" upon which he was booed by the Washington press corps. The incident was widely reported by the national media outlets.

On June 5, 1985, Greg spoke to the Third Generation on "Why Conservatives Are Winning Intellectually, Politically, and Culturally."

CONSTANCE (CONNIE) HECKMAN: Born in 1955, Connie is a native of Long Island, New York, and chose the Reagan, as opposed to the Ford, wing of the Republican Party in 1976, when she served as chairman of New York Youth for Reagan. She also participated in the Republican National Conventions on the Reagan side in both 1976 and 1980. In 1978 she joined the staff of the American Legislative Exchange Council (ALEC), whose focus is policy and legislation at the state level. It is her belief that many of the most important issues that affect our lives are settled by the states, an area that has largely been ignored by conservatives until recently. While at ALEC, Connie held the position of assistant executive director and director of research. Her primary responsibilities included publications, conferences, and special projects. In 1979, Connie served as director of *The 1980 Source Book* project, a compendium of suggested state legislation often referred to by state legislators throughout the country.

In 1981, Connie left ALEC to become the intergovernmental affairs director of the federal volunteer agency, ACTION. She then went on to become the legislative director for Republican Mickey Edwards, the congressman from Oklahoma and chairman of the American Conservative Union.

In 1984, Connie accepted a position under Elizabeth Dole as special assistant at the U.S. Department of Transportation, where her responsibilities included issue management, event planning, and policy development and coordination. In June of 1985, she was offered, and accepted, the executive directorship of ALEC, her former employer, and now directs all its activities. She is also a member of the board of directors of the Fund for a Conservative Majority-State Fund.

Connie is married to Robert Heckman, former Chairman of the Fund for a Conservative Majority and now the executive director of Jack Kemp's political action committee, Campaign for Prosperity.

On May 7, 1986, Connie spoke to the Third Generation on "Why State Politics is Crucial for Continuing the Conservative Revolution."

LAURA INGRAHAM: Born in 1963, Laura Ingraham is a speechwriter and confidential assistant to the White House domestic policy adviser, Gary Bauer.

Graduating from Dartmouth College in 1985 with honors in English literature, Laura was editor-in-chief of both *The Dartmouth Review* and *Prospect* magazine at Princeton University.

She grew up in Glastonbury, Connecticut, a small town near Hartford, acquiring her conservative instincts at an early age. At *The Dartmouth Review,* her instincts were refined and given an avenue of expression. Laura rose quickly through the ranks to become its first female editor.

In the summer of 1983, she studied for six months at the University of Leningrad where she observed first-hand how communism "destroys the human impulse to be creative and enjoy life." In the summer of 1985, she studied journalism and political philosophy as a Publius fellow at Public Research Syndicated, in Claremont, California. While still an undergraduate, Laura's articles appeared in such national publications as *Human Events* and *The American Spectator*. Since then, her work has been published in *National Review, Policy Review, The Detroit News,* and *People* magazine.

On April 23, 1986, Laura spoke to the Third Generation on "What the Third Generation Can Learn from the Left."

MICHAEL JOHNS: Born in 1964, Mike Johns gained national notice when he founded the *Miami Tribune* in 1983 while a student at the University of Miami. *The Los Angeles Times* labeled Johns's newspaper "one of the three most successful" conservative campus publications in America. Mike was awarded the James Brady Award as "the most outstanding student journalist in America" for his lambasting of the university establishment for liberal bias in the classrooms. *The Miami Tribune* earned more than $50,000 a year from advertising revenue alone, which allowed the conservative paper to publish weekly. Johns graduated from the University of Miami with honors in economics and went on to study literature at Cambridge University in England.

In January of 1984, Johns, along with Michael Waller, traveled with the anti-communist resistance who are fighting the Sandinista government in Nicaragua. Since then, Johns has reported from the Middle East and the Soviet Union.

A graduate of the National Journalism Center in Washington, Mike was a Capitol Hill reporter for *Human Events*. He has written for *Chronicles of Culture, The Washington Times, Diario Las Americas, South African Digest,* and other publications. He is now assistant editor of *Policy Review,* The Heritage Foundation's quarterly journal, and is working on a book about Nicaragua.

On September 17, 1985, Mike Johns spoke to the Third Generation on "The Fallacy of Negotiation with the Sandinistas."

ROY JONES: Born in 1959, Roy Jones is senior vice president of political affairs for the Liberty Federation, formerly the Moral Majority. Prior to his promotion in June of 1986, he was the Moral Majority's director of legislative affairs. Roy first came to the attention of the Reverend Jerry Falwell when, as an undergraduate at Liberty University in Lynchburg, Virginia, he founded a 600-member chapter of Young Americans for Freedom, the largest YAF chapter in the country.

Roy is also the founder of the Conservative Youth Federation of America, the coordinator for the Coalition for Religious Liberties, and a visiting lecturer for the American University's Washington Semester Program. Roy coordinated the campaign of Governor Meldrim Thomson's reelection effort in New Hampshire, in addition to independent expenditure campaigns for the Fund for a Conservative Majority in New Hampshire and South Carolina on behalf of then presidential candidate Ronald Reagan.

Although Roy runs a legislative office for the Liberty Federation in Washington, D.C., he considers his real home to be Lynchburg, Virginia, where he lives with his wife Melinda and their two children.

Roy spoke to the Third Generation group on August 21, 1985, on "Religion, Moral Issues, and Politics."

WILLIAM KEYES: Born in 1953, the cut-off year for Third Generation membership, Bill Keyes served from 1981 to 1984 as a senior policy analyst on President Reagan's White House staff. Before joining the White House, he was a staff economist on the Joint Economic Committee of the U.S. Congress.

Since leaving government in 1983, Bill has founded Black PAC, an organization that specializes in assisting and teaching conservative candidates for national office how to win support from black voters. He also began his own consulting business, International Public Affairs Consultants, Inc., whose list of clients include South Africa. Bill has always believed that disinvestment from South Africa would be disastrous to the black population and that a takeover of the country by the radical African National Congress would lead to a blood bath. His hope is that the South African government will encourage the moderate elements of the black South African community, such as Inkatha, the largest black South African political organization, whose leader, Chief Mangosuthu Gatsha Buthelezi, opposes both apartheid and U.S. sanctions.

Bill has written many articles and columns on domestic policy issues—from the minimum wage and the Davis-Bacon Act to tuition tax credits and education vouchers. His columns and articles have appeared in numerous publications, including *The Washington Post, The Washington Times, The Chicago Tribune,* and *The Philadelphia Inquirer.* He is a contributing editor for *Conservative Digest* and *Lincoln Review.*

His article advocating repeal of the Davis-Bacon Act, published in *The Journal of Labor Research,* has been reprinted several times in the *Congressional Record* and has been used as expert testimony during congressional consideration of the Act.

Bill has been the subject of many feature articles, including one in *The Washington Post,* and has appeared on many network television and radio shows to comment on events in South Africa as well as to discuss why black Americans should embrace conservative ideas.

On August 8, 1984, Bill spoke to the Third Generation on "Blacks and Conservatives: How the Third Generation Can Mend the Division."

FRANK LAVIN: Born in 1957, Frank Lavin serves as deputy executive secretary of the National Security Council at the White House, where he is responsible for coordinating presidential meetings and trips. Previously, he served as associate director of the White House Office of Public Liaison and has worked in other White House offices. Frank also worked in the Asian and African bureau of the State Department.

A philologist by training, Frank majored in international politics at the School of Foreign Service at Georgetown University. He went on to do graduate studies at National Taiwan Normal University, Johns Hopkins University, and Georgetown University, from which he received an M.A. in Chinese. He has published articles in such publications as *The Wall Street Journal* and *The Washington Monthly.*

On October 3, 1984, he spoke to the Third Generation on "Realignment Issues for the Third Generation."

DAVID MASON: Born in 1958, Dave Mason began his political career at age six, passing out bumper stickers for Barry Goldwater in 1964. He went on to become the founding chairman of the Lynchburg College Republican club in 1975.

Dave has been a delegate to the Virginia State Republican Conventions from 1976 through 1985, and he began his Capitol Hill career in 1978 as an intern to Congressman Caldwell Butler, a Virginia Republican. That same year he took a job as assistant director of research for Obenshain/Warner for the U.S. Senate. Dave became a legislative assistant to Senator John Warner in 1979, and from there he went on to become the legislative director for Republican Congressman Thomas Bliley of Virginia. In 1983, he took over the chairmanship of the Arlington County Young Republicans.

After four years as Congressman Bliley's Legislative Director, Dave became a key player in the House leadership as the staff director for the House of Representatives' Whip office, held by Congressman Trent Lott, the Republican from Mississippi. Dave held that position for two years, and in 1986 founded his own political consulting firm, which does research and writing for state-wide and national political campaigns and conservative political organizations, including Americans for Tax Reform.

Dave is a recent convert to the Roman Catholic Church. He and his wife, Margaret, and their two children, live in Lynchburg, Virginia. He hopes to run for public office.

On September 12, 1984, he spoke to the Third Generation on "Why Conservatives Need Religious Issues in Order to Win."

PATRICK MCGUIGAN: Born in 1954, Pat McGuigan is editor of the *Initiative and Referendum Report,* a newsletter with the best information available on direct democracy in which the people vote "yes" or "no" on a particular piece of legislation. A well-known example is Proposition 13 in California, in which the people voted to slash property taxes. Pat believes that direct democracy, if used properly, can become a weapon for the conservative cause. He authored a book on the subject entitled *The Politics of Direct Democracy in the 1980s: Case Studies in Popular Decision Making,* published by the Institute for Government and Politics, which is under McGuigan's direction.

Pat also directs the Institute's judicial reform project, an ongoing research effort of Paul Weyrich's Free Congress Foundation. In this capacity, Pat played a key role in the nomination of Edwin Meese for Attorney General, and Pat has spearheaded efforts to nominate such conservative judges as Antonin Scalia to the Supreme Court, William Rehnquist as the nation's Chief Justice, and Dan Manion as President Reagan's choice to sit on the 7th U.S. Circuit Court of Appeals. Manion, one of the most conservative of all Reagan's judicial appointments, thanked Pat in a letter for his "magnificent" effort "through this difficult nomination process." Manion's letter continued: "Simply said, without your coordinating the campaign against all the liberal attacks, I would not have had a chance." The letter fell into the hands of Norman Lear's People for the American Way, which tried to make it an issue. The effort was too late, however, as Manion had already been confirmed.

Pat is generally considered one of the most knowledgeable of conservative activists on judicial matters. He edited *A Blueprint for Judicial Reform* (1981) and *Criminal Justice Reform: A Blueprint* (1983), two studies credited with providing the intellectual foundation for many of the reforms included in the Comprehensive Crime Control Act of 1984, considered a major landmark for conservative legislation to mandate stiff sentencing for violent crimes.

He has authored hundreds of articles on direct democracy, congressional races, family policy, criminal justice, judicial reform, and legal policy for such publications as *The Wall Street Journal, The Los Angeles Times, The Washington Times,* and *Policy Review.* He is a contributing editor for *Conservative Digest* and has edited five books on legal policy questions.

Pat is a graduate of Oklahoma State University and has an M.A. in medieval history from the same institution. He lives in Arlington, Virginia, with his wife Pamela and their four children.

On August 7, 1985, Pat spoke to the Third Generation on "New Frontiers for the Third Generation: Direct Democracy and Judicial Reform."

LEIGH ANN METZGER: Born in 1962, Leigh Ann Metzger grew up in a conservative family and was prodded to become an activist after seeing the distorted picture of the world presented in the national media. She became disgusted with the "value-free" approach of most journalists to the news—their failing, for example, to acknowledge a moral difference between a free and democratic United States and a totalitarian Soviet Union.

A graduate of Sanford University in Birmingham, Alabama, with a B.A. in political science, Leigh Ann's first job in Washington was with conservative freshman Congressman Pat Swindall of Georgia. She took the position after working in Georgia for the Reagan-Bush 1984 Presidential campaign where she organized phone banks and mail drops for three states.

Leigh Ann went on to become legislative director for Phyllis Schlafly's Eagle Forum. Since joining that group in 1985, Leigh Ann has worked to put together coalitions to combat "dangerous" comparable worth legislation, which, if passed, would leave the setting of salaries up to government bureaucrats rather than the market. "It would bring us socialism through the back door," says Leigh Ann, who also has worked to pass tax reform legislation that would lower rates, and to persuade family stores to stop selling pornography. She spends much of her energy alerting law enforcement officials about existing laws against the distributing of hard-core porn.

For several months in 1986, Leigh Ann took a leave of absence from Eagle Forum to direct the Pornography Commission Report Project. The aim of the project was to combat distortions in the press and to present to the voting public the correct information regarding the Justice Department's report on pornography. Since there was no other conservative group in the Washington area working on pornography, Leigh Ann saw a need for an information clearinghouse on the issue. As director of the project, she sent out press releases with news of the Pornography Commission's findings, set up press conferences, and made herself available to answer questions from reporters. The project has been concluded, and she has returned to the Eagle Forum as legislative director.

On July 23, 1986, Leigh Ann spoke to the Third Generation on "Pornography: Indecency versus Obscenity."

ADAM MEYERSON: Born in 1953, Adam Meyerson is the editor of *Policy Review,* The Heritage Foundation's quarterly journal. Previously, he was an editorial writer for *The Wall Street Journal* and managing editor of *The American Spectator.* He is also co-editor of *The Wall Street Journal on Management.* Adam, a *summa cum laude* graduate of Yale University, majoring in history and the arts and letters, wrote his thesis on Adam Smith's *Wealth of Nations* and Edmund Burke's *Reflections on the Revolution in France,* two seminal works for conservatives. He was also a doctoral student in international business at Harvard Business School before joining *The Wall Street Journal.*

Adam comes from an intellectual, liberal family. His father was president of the University of Pennsylvania. But Adam, heavily influenced by R. Emmett Tyrrell while working at *The American Spectator,* found himself arriving at conservative conclusions after examining the data on liberal policy prescriptions. Moreover, conservative conclusions seemed to be justified even under liberal assumptions. Charles Murray's *Losing Ground* appealed to Adam's empirical way of thinking. Murray, no conservative himself when he began his book on the effects of poverty programs on the poor, looked at the evidence and concluded Lyndon Johnson's Great Society was a cataclysmic failure. "The programs failed even if we use the liberals' own criteria," says Adam.

Adam has brought his empirical approach to *Policy Review,* where he demands facts before ideology in promoting or debunking a policy proposal. He is willing to publish a risky or zany article, as long as the thesis is supported by hard data and sound reasoning. An example was an article by Richard Rahn, an economist at the U.S.

Chamber of Commerce, who proposed the privatization of money. Adam thought the article made sense, and ran it.

On April 11, 1984, Adam spoke to the Third Generation on "Reagan's Foreign Policy Revolution."

AMY MORITZ: Born in 1959, Amy Moritz has been involved in conservative politics for almost ten years, on the local level in Pennsylvania and Maryland, and on the national level, working for the Republican National Committee and the Reagan-Bush campaign in 1980. She is currently the executive director of the National Center for Public Policy Research in Washington, D.C., a position she has held since 1982. In this capacity, she directs educational efforts on foreign policy, economics, and social issues. She works with other conservative groups to mobilize grass-roots America to support conservative ideas and protest liberal notions as they come up in Congress. Her organization is affectionately referred to by conservatives as "rent a riot," because of the speed with which she can mobilize a crowd in front of the Soviet embassy to protest Soviet atrocities.

Amy also serves as director of The Enterprise Foundation, national chairman of the Conservative Youth Federation of America, one of four founding members of Liberty International, and as a member of the board of advisors of several conservative organizations, capacities in which she directs the political activities of young people. Amy was also employed by the Western Goals Foundation of Alexandria, Virginia, then under the leadership of the late Representative Lawrence P. McDonald.

Amy was awarded the William Paca Award for the Most Outstanding Young Republican in Maryland in May 1978.

Most recently, she became a founding member of the board of directors of the Conservative Student Support Foundation and joined the board of directors of Accuracy in Academia.

On February 14, 1984, Amy spoke to the Third Generation on "How to Mobilize the Third Generation."

DEROY MURDOCK: Born in 1963, Deroy Murdock, a native of Los Angeles, has been developing as a conservative since junior high school. By observing the policies of President Jimmy Carter, he began to see the dangers of modern liberalism. In 1978, he followed the trial of Soviet dissident Anatoly Scharansky and learned that communism is evil, and that the Soviet Union poses the greatest danger to freedom and democracy in the world.

When he was 16, Deroy joined the 1980 Reagan presidential campaign. While a student at Georgetown University, he spent three years on the staff of Senator Orrin Hatch, the Republican from Utah, and was an officer of the 1984 Republican National Convention. Deroy was also active in Young Americans for Freedom, serving on the organization's national board and as chairman of its Washington, D.C., chapter.

Articles by Deroy have appeared in *Policy Review, The Washington Times,* and *Human Events.* He has lectured at Dartmouth College and Howard University. He has been a guest on the *Phil Donahue Show, Today Show,* and *Morningbreak,* making the case for why black Americans should support conservatives for elected office. Deroy was also the subject of a front page feature in *The Washington Post*'s "Style" section, which focused on his conservative activism at Georgetown University, where he was a vocal opponent of U.S. sanctions against South Africa.

Deroy graduated *cum laude* from Georgetown in 1986, and is pursuing an MBA at New York University's Graduate School of Business Administration.

On July 10, 1985, Deroy spoke to the Third Generation on "Why Conservative Ideas Should Appeal to Young Black Americans." He also delivered, on October 22, 1985, "A Tribute to Barry Goldwater by the Third Generation" at a banquet sponsored by The Heritage Foundation in honor of the retiring Senator from Arizona.

GROVER NORQUIST: Born in 1956, Grover Norquist graduated from Harvard University with a degree in economics in 1978. He also has an M.B.A. from the Harvard Business School, from which he graduated in 1981.

In the interim between college and business school, Grover was the executive director of the National Taxpayers Union, where he was active in fifteen state-wide initiatives to cut taxes and limit spending. During his tenure, the balanced budget constitutional amendment received the endorsement of eighteen state legislatures, bringing the number of states calling for a constitutional convention to 30, four short of the required 34.

After graduating from Harvard Business School, Grover became executive director of the College Republican National Committee and, in his eight month tenure, he helped build the organization from virtual nonexistence to more than 800 campus clubs. Grover is considered by many to be an expert in grass-roots political organization.

Grover went on to become the chief speechwriter for the United States Chamber of Commerce for two years, during which time he also served as an economist for the U.S. Chamber's Economic Policy Division.

Grover was then hired as the national field director for

Citizens for America (CFA), a grass-roots organization founded by Lew Lehrman to lobby for President Reagan's agenda. While at CFA, Grover helped organize the campaign in support of U.S. assistance to the freedom fighters in Nicaragua and the campaign to build the MX missile. He also attended a meeting in Jamba, Angola, where freedom fighters from Cambodia, Angola, Nicaragua, and Afghanistan met. They signed the Jamba Accord, drafted by Grover, pledging solidarity to the cause of removing Soviet-backed dictatorships from their respective countries. Grover has since made a number of trips to Angola, and he is currently at work on a book about Jonas Savimbi, leader of Angola's anti-communist UNITA movement, which has 65,000 armed troops.

Grover was also president of Americans for Tax Reform, a grass-roots lobby dedicated to lowering tax rates in order to permit economic expansion favorable to the average American family. One of Grover's campaigns was to encourage as many members of Congress as possible to sign a pledge promising: 1) Never to vote for an increase in marginal tax rates and 2) Never to vote for an elimination of tax deductions unless matched dollar-for-dollar by further reducing tax rates. Any member of Congress who fails to sign the "no tax increase" pledge leaves himself vulnerable on the major issue that sunk the Mondale campaign.

On July 25, 1984, Grover spoke to the Third Generation on "Building the Conservative Movement for Tomorrow."

WALTER OLSON: Born in 1954, Walter Olson is vice president for research at the Manhattan Institute for Policy Research in New York City, and directs its project for Civil Justice Reform. Before that, he spent five years at the American Enterprise Institute as associate editor of the magazine

Regulation. He has also worked for the House Republican Research Committee and for the National Journalism Center.

A graduate of Yale University, where he was a member of Yale's Party of the Right, Walter considers himself a libertarian-conservative—meaning he holds a libertarian philosophy, but thinks the Libertarian Party painfully irrelevant. "The best way for libertarian views to have an impact on policy," says Walter, "is for libertarians to join the conservatives."

On March 14, 1984, Walter spoke to the Third Generation on "The Role of Libertarians in the Third Generation."

JOSEPH PERKINS: Born in 1958, Joseph Perkins was, along with Greg Fossedal, one of the two youngest editorial writers ever hired by *The Wall Street Journal.* Joseph attended Howard University in Washington, D.C., and graduated in 1984 with honors from the City College of New York. He first caught the eye of *Journal* editor Robert Bartley when, as a student, Joseph duplicated the format of *The Wall Street Journal* as editor of the student newspaper at Howard. More startling than the fact that the Howard paper looked like *The Wall Street Journal* was that the campus publication read like the *Journal,* complete with sophisticated economic analysis, free market editorial positions, and the promotion of tax cuts as the best way to spur economic growth. Joseph was undeterred when Howard University students and professors staged demonstrations outside his editorial offices and wrote scathing letters to the editor in protest of Perkins's unabashedly pro-capitalist positions.

On April 3, 1985, Joseph spoke to the Third Generation

about "The Rising Conservative Tide Among Young Black Americans."

RALPH REED, JR.: Born in 1961, in Portsmouth, Virginia, Ralph Reed was junior and senior class president and was selected "most likely to succeed" by the class of 1979 of Stephens County High School. He also served on the varsity debate team, was an Eagle Scout and junior assistant scoutmaster, and was chosen "most outstanding young statesman in America" by the Young Men's Christian Association.

After working on his first U.S. congressional campaign at the age of 14, Ralph served as an intern in the office of the lieutenant governor of Georgia in 1980. He was elected chairman of the College Republicans of the University of Georgia, where he actively worked on the campaigns of Ronald Reagan for President and Mack Mattingly for U.S. Senate. Following Mattingly's stunning upset of Herman Talmadge, Georgia's senior senator, Ralph served as a staff assistant in Senator Mattingly's office in Washington.

Elected state chairman of the College Republicans of Georgia in 1982, Ralph later served as executive director of the College Republican National Committee (1982–1984) and presided over the Southern Area College Republican convention in 1982. During his tenure at the CRNC, the national College Republican membership soared to over 100,000 with an annual budget of $600,000.

On March 9–11, 1984, Ralph presided over the founding conference of Students for America at the Rock Castle Conference Center in Powhatan, Virginia. Students for America is a patriotic, conservative student group dedicated to the advancement of Judeo-Christian values among America's youth. Since its founding, Students for America has enjoyed the distinction of being the fastest growing political youth group in the nation. Today it has approximately 10,000 members on roughly 200 campuses in 41 states and an annual budget of $100,000. Headquartered in Raleigh, North Carolina, Students for America played a central role in the reelection of Senator Jesse Helms in 1984.

Ralph is currently a Ph.D. candidate in American history at Emory University in Atlanta. He is a published author, and was awarded for the most outstanding senior history thesis by the University of Georgia in 1983. He also received the Benjamin and McDobbs Prizes by Emory University for being an outstanding master's student and for writing the most outstanding research paper by a history graduate student.

Ralph spoke to the Third Generation on "How Christian Revival is Changing American Politics."

TERRY TEACHOUT: Born in 1956 in Cape Girardeau, Missouri, Terry Teachout is a senior editor of *Harper's* and one of the very few conservatives on the magazine's staff. His interest is culture, more than policy, and he fears that conservatives are falling into the liberal trap of believing that everything will be fine if only we implement the right policy. "As conservatives," says Terry, "we know there are social problems out there that cannot be fixed. The main social problem, of course, is Original Sin." Terry worries that the "feel-good" politics of the 1980s might backfire against conservatives when the nation encounters bad times. "I am most definitely not a libertarian," he says.

Terry writes about television for *National Review,* frequently reviews books for *Commentary* and *The American Spectator,* and writes about classical music for *High Fidelity.* Recently, he started publishing a conservative newsletter, *Modern Times,* which comments on new cultural and intellectual currents within the baby boom generation.

He attended St. Johns College, William Jewell College, and the University of Illinois at Urbana-Champaign. He is a founding editor of the *Illinios Review,* a conservative student monthly. Terry lives in New York with his wife Elizabeth, an opera coach and accompanist.

On December 19, 1985, Terry Teachout spoke to the Third Generation on the question: "Will Optimism Be the Death of the Conservative Movement?"

RICHARD VIGILANTE: Born in 1956, Richard Vigilante joined *National Review* in 1985 as executive editor in charge of articles. Before that he worked as an editorial writer for the *Charleston Daily Mail* in West Virginia and then *The Washington Times.* He is also a writer and producer of political documentaries, his most recent being "Born in the U.S.A.," which is about immigration and is narrated by George Gilder. The show was broadcast on PBS.

Rich is a graduate of Yale University where he was chairman of the Party of the Right, which is both a debating society and a major recruiting ground for the Reagan Administration. He is also a graduate of Stan Evans's National Journalism Center in Washington, which has been responsible for placing dozens of conservative journalists and editors in important editorial positions in the media.

After graduating from the National Journalism Center's program, his first editorial position was as the Washington editor of *Consumers Research,* also under the direction of Stan Evans, where he edited a compendium entitled *Consumer Issues for the 1980s* on how federal regulations plague consumers. He co-authored *Grenada: The Untold Story* and was a consultant to the White House outreach group on Central America.

Rich arrived at his conservative perspective through his upbringing as a Roman Catholic, which taught him that there are certain immutable truths one must live by. "Once you accept that there is a higher moral order governing our destiny," says Rich, "it becomes more difficult to accept the claims of the state as absolute."

On November 20, 1985, Richard spoke to the Third Generation on "The Third Generation as a New Intellectual Movement."

MICHAEL WALLER: Mike Waller was born in 1962. He founded *The Sequent* while he was a student at George Washington University, where he specialized in exposing the radical Left activities of his professors. Mike Waller and Michael Johns were the first American student journalists to travel with the Nicaraguan Democratic Force (FDN) resistance fighters in Central America. Graduating Phi Beta Kappa in 1985 with a degree in international affairs, Mike went on to become director of publications at the Council for Inter-American Security in Washington.

He is editor of the newsletters *Westwatch* and *Freedom Fighter,* both containing information mainly about Central America. In addition, he edits *New Guard,* the magazine published by Young Americans for Freedom. He also co-authored the book *The Revolution Lobby,* detailing the Washington-based network of political groups lobbying Capitol Hill on behalf of communist movements in Central America and the Caribbean.

On October 1, 1986, Mike spoke to the Third Generation about "The Revolution Lobby in Washington."

PETER YOUNG: Born in 1961, Peter Young is executive director of the Adam Smith Institute's new U.S. branch in Washington, D.C. Before opening up his Washington office, Peter was the director of research for the Adam Smith Institute in London, the major British public policy think tank relied on by Margaret Thatcher's Administration and one of the pioneers of the strategy of privatization, which seeks to transfer government functions to the private sector. Peter directed the Institute's Omega project, which produced fifteen separate reports containing privatization proposals for every area of government. Many of these proposals have been adopted by the Thatcher government, including plans to shift Britain's version of Social Security into private hands, the deregulation and privatization of road transportation, requirements to privatize local government services, and the selling of British airports, the post office, and the electric power industry to the private sector.

In the U.S., Peter has advised the U.S. Office of Personnel Management and the Department of the Interior on their privatization strategies and has traveled to the South Pacific advising governments on their privatization efforts. Peter specializes in the development of politically acceptable privatization strategies tailor-made for particular situations.

He has also written widely on privatization, and his work has been published by such organizations as The Heritage Foundation, the Cato Institute, the National Center for Policy Analysis, and the Adam Smith Institute. His articles have appeared in *The New York Times, The Wall Street Journal, U.S. News and World Report, Government and Union Review,* and *Human Events.*

Some of his publications include "The Omega File,"

"Privatizing America," and "Aiding Development," all published by the Adam Smith Institute; "Privatization Lessons from Britain," "Saving Social Security: Lessons from Britain," and "Privatizing the Third World," published by The Heritage Foundation; "Privatization Worldwide," published by the Academy of Political Science as part of a book on privatization; "Privatization: The Worker Buy-Out Option," published by the Cato Institute; and "Privatization Around the Globe: Lessons for the Reagan Administration," published by the National Center for Policy Analysis.

On July 10, 1985, Peter spoke to the Third Generation on "Lessons President Reagan Can Learn from Margaret Thatcher."

A CONSERVATIVE HERITAGE

Conservatives believe strongly in building upon the thought and experiences of the past. A good example of this is the debate over the adoption of the Constitution of the United States with Alexander Hamilton and James Madison quoting extensively from thinkers ranging from Aristotle to Montesquieu to make their arguments and develop their views. Similarly, the Third Generation relies heavily on those who came before, both for intellectual ammunition and organization of resources. The following list of titles comprises part of this heritage inherited by the Third Generation. This selected bibliography is divided into four categories: *First Generation, Second Generation,* and *Third Generation* books as well as works that can be considered *Classics.* Taken together, these works do not form a uniform, tightly packaged ideology but, rather, are representative of a wide range of conservative thought. Some books, in fact, are intended as direct rebuttals of others also included on this list. Russell Kirk and Friedrich Hayek, for example, had highly publicized disagreements, as did Peter Viereck and Frank Meyer. But the works included below can fairly be said to represent a broadly conservative view of the world.

FIRST GENERATION BOOKS

Arendt, Hannah. *Origins of Totalitarianism.* Reprinted from 1951 edition. New York: Harcourt, Brace and Jovanovich, 1973.

Babbitt, Irving. *Democracy and Leadership.* Reprinted from 1924 edition. Indianapolis: Liberty Classics, 1979.

Belloc, Hilaire. *The Servile State.* Reprinted from 1913 edition. Indianapolis: Liberty Classics, 1977.

Berns, Walter. *After the People Vote.* Washington, D.C.: American Enterprise Institute, 1983.

—*The First Amendment and the Future of American Democracy.* New York: Basic Books, 1985.

—*Freedom, Virtue and the First Amendment.* Reprinted from 1957 edition. Westport, Conn.: Greenwood Press, 1978.

Buchanan, James M. *The Economics of Politics.* Albuquerque: Transatlantic, 1979.

Buchanan, James M. and Robert D. Tollison. *The Theory of Public Choice*, 2 vols. Ann Arbor: University of Michigan Press, 1972 and 1984.

Buchanan, James M. and Gordon Tullock. *The Calculus of Consent: Logical Foundations of Constitutional Democracy.* Ann Arbor: University of Michigan Press, 1962.

Buchanan, James M., and Richard E. M. Wagner. *Democracy in Deficit: The Political Legacy of Lord Keynes.* New York: Academic Press, 1977.

Buckley, William F., Jr., editor. *Did You Ever See a Dream Walking: American Conservative Thought in the Twentieth Century.* New York: Bobbs-Merrill Co., 1970.

—*God and Man at Yale: The Superstitions of "Academic Freedom."* Revised from 1951 edition. Chicago: Regnery Gateway, 1977.

—*Up From Liberalism.* Revised from 1959 edition. New York: Stein and Day, 1984.

Buckley, William F., Jr. and Brent L. Bozell. *McCarthy and His Enemies.* Chicago: Regnery Gateway, 1954.

Burnham, James. *Containment or Liberation.* New York: John Day Co., 1953.

—*The Struggle for the World.* New York: John Day Co., 1947.

—*Suicide of the West: An Essay on the Meaning and Destiny of Liberalism.* Reprinted from 1964 edition. Chicago: Regnery Gateway, 1985.

—*The War We Are In.* New Rochelle, N.Y.: Arlington House Publishers, 1967.

Chamberlain, John. *The Roots of Capitalism.* Indianapolis: Liberty Press, 1981.

Chambers, Whittaker. *Witness.* Reprinted from 1952 edition. Chicago: Regnery Gateway, 1978.

Chesterton, G.K. *Orthodoxy.* Reprinted from 1908 edition. Westport, Conn.: Greenwood Press, 1974.

Chodorov, Frank. *One Is a Crowd.* New York: Devin-Adair Co., 1952.

Crossman, Richard, editor. *The God that Failed.* Reprinted from 1950 edition. Chicago: Regnery Gateway, 1983.

Davidson, Donald. *The Attack on Leviathan: Regionalism and Nationalism in the United States.* Chapel Hill: University of North Carolina Press, 1938.

Dietze, Gottfried. *In Defense of Property.* Translated from 1963 edition. Baltimore: Johns Hopkins University Press, 1971.

Eastman, Max. *Marxism: Is It Science?* New York: W.W. Norton & Co., 1940.

—*Reflections on the Failure of Socialism.* New York: Devin-Adair Co., 1955.

Eliot, T.S. *Christianity and Culture.* Including two essays, "The Idea of a Christian Society" and "Notes Toward the Definition of Culture." New York: Harcourt, Brace and Jovanovich, 1980.

Friedman, Milton. *Capitalism and Freedom.* Chicago: University of Chicago Press, 1962.

Friedman, Milton and Rose Friedman. *Free to Choose.* New York: Harcourt, Brace and Jovanovich, 1980.

—*Tyranny of the Status Quo.* New York: Harcourt, Brace and Jovanovich, 1984.

Gasset, Jose Ortega. *The Revolt of the Masses.* Translated from 1930 edition. New York: W.W. Norton & Co., 1957.

Goldwater, Barry. *The Conscience of a Conservative.* Shepherdsville, Kentucky: Victor Publishing Co., 1960.

Hayek, Friedrich. *The Constitution of Liberty.* Reprinted from 1960 edition. Regnery Gateway, 1972.

—*Law, Legislation and Liberty*, 3 vols. Chicago: University of Chicago Press, 1978.
—*The Road to Serfdom*. Chicago: University of Chicago Press, 1944.
Hazlitt, Henry. *Economics in One Lesson*. Revised from 1946 edition. New Rochelle: Arlington House Publishers, 1979.
—*The Failure of the "New Economics": An Analysis of the Keynesian Fallacies*. Princeton, N.J.: D. Van Nostrand Co., 1959.
—*The Foundations of Morality*. Revised from 1964 edition. Fairfax, Va.: Institute for Humane Studies, 1980.
—*Man vs. the Welfare State*. New Rochelle: Arlington House Publishers, 1970.
Hoffer, Eric. *The True Believer*. Reprinted from 1951 edition. New York: Harper & Row Publishers, 1976.
Hogg, Quintin. *The Case for Conservatism*. Harmondsworth, Middlesex, England: Penguin, 1947.
Hook, Sidney. *The Paradoxes of Freedom*. Revised from 1970 edition. Westport, Conn.: Greenwood Press, 1984.
Hoover, Herbert. *American Individualism*. Garden City, N.Y.: Doubleday, 1922.
—*Challenge to Liberty*. New York: Charles Scribner's Sons, 1934.
Hutt, W.H. *Keynesianism: Retrospect and Prospect*. Chicago: Regnery Gateway, 1963.
—*A Rehabilitation of Say's Law*. Athens: Ohio University Press, 1975.
—*The Theory of Collective Bargaining*. Reprinted from 1954 edition. Albuquerque: Transatlantic, 1976.
Huxley, Aldous. *Brave New World*. Reprinted from 1932 edition. New York: Harper and Row, 1979.
Jouvenel, Bertrand de. *On Power*. Translated from 1945 edition. Boston: Beacon Press, 1962.
Kendall, Willmoore. *The Conservative Affirmation*. Reprinted from 1963 edition. Chicago: Regnery Gateway, 1985.
—*Contra Mundum*. New Rochelle: Arlington House Publishers, 1971.
Kendall, Willmoore and George W. Carey. *Basic Symbols of the American Political Tradition*. Baton Rouge: Louisiana State University Press, 1970.

Kirk, Russell. *The Conservative Mind: From Burke to Eliot.* Revised from 1953 edition. Chicago: Regnery Gateway, 1978.
—*Eliot and His Age.* Reprinted from 1972 edition. La Salle, Ill.: Sherwood Sugden & Co., 1984.
—*Enemies of the Permanent Things.* New Rochelle: Arlington House Publishers, 1969.
—*The Intelligent Women's Guide to Conservatism.* New York: Devin-Adair Co., 1957.
—editor. *The Portable Conservative Reader.* East Rutherford, N.J.: Viking Penguin 1982.
—*Roots of American Order.* La Salle, Ill.: Open Court Publishing Co., 1974.
Knight, Frank Hyneman. *The Ethics of Competition.* Reprinted from 1935 edition. New York: Augustus M. Kelley Publishers, 1951.
Koestler, Arthur. *Darkness at Noon.* Reprinted from 1941 edition. New York: Macmillan Publishing Co., 1967.
Kravchenko, Victor. *I Chose Freedom.* New York: Charles Scribner's Sons, 1946.
Kuenhelt-Leddihn, Erik von. *Liberty or Equality.* Caldwell, Idaho: Caxton Printers, Ltd., 1952.
Lane, Rose Wilder. *The Discovery of Freedom.* New York: John Day Co., 1943.
Lewis, C.S. *Mere Christianity.* New York: Macmillan Publishing Co, 1964.
Lippman, Walter. *The Good Society.* Reprinted from 1937 edition. Westport, Conn.: Greenwood Press, 1973.
Manion, Clarence. *The Key to Peace.* Chicago: Heritage Foundation, 1950.
Maritain, Jacques. *Man and the State.* Chicago: University of Chicago Press, 1956.
Meyer, Frank S. *In Defense of Freedom.* Chicago: Regnery Gateway, 1962.
—editor. *What is Conservatism?* New York: Holt, Rinehart & Winston, 1964.
Milosz, Czeslaw. *The Captive Mind.* New York: Alfred A. Knopf, Inc., 1953.

Mises, Ludwig von. *Bureaucracy.* New Haven: Yale University Press, 1944.
—*Human Action: A Treatise on Economics.* Revised from 1949 edition. Chicago: Regnery Gateway, 1966.
—*Omnipotent Government.* New Haven: Yale University Press, 1944.
—*Socialism.* Reprinted from 1936 edition. Indianapolis: Liberty Classics, 1981.
Molnar, Thomas. *The Counter Revolution.* New York: Funk & Wagnalls Co., 1969.
—*The Future of Education.* New York: Fleet Press Corp., 1970.
Morley, Felix. *Freedom and Federalism.* Chicago: Regnery Gateway, 1959.
—*The Power in the People.* Princeton: D. Van Nostrand Co, 1949.
Murray, John Courtney, S.J. *We Hold These Truths: Catholic Reflections on the American Proposition.* New York: Sheed and Ward, 1960.
Niemeyer, Gerhart. *Between Nothingness and Paradise.* Baton Rouge: Louisiana State University Press, 1971.
Nisbet, Robert. *Conservatism: Dream and Reality.* Minneapolis: University of Minnesota Press, 1986.
—*The Quest for Community.* Revised from 1953 edition. New York: Oxford University Press, 1962.
—*Tradition and Revolt.* Revised from 1952 edition. New York: Vintage Books, 1970.
—*Twilight of Authority.* New York: Oxford University Press, 1975.
Nock, Albert J. *Memoirs of a Superfluous Man.* Reprinted from 1943 edition. Chicago: Regnery Gateway, 1964.
—*Our Enemy the State.* New York: William Morrow & Co., 1935.
Oakeshott, Michael. *Rationalism in Politics.* New York: Basic Books, 1962.
Orwell, George. *Animal Farm.* Reprinted from 1946 edition. New York: Signet Classics, 1974.
—*Nineteen Eighty-Four.* New York: Harcourt Brace, 1949.
Pei, Mario. *The America We Lost: The Concerns of a Conservative.* Reprinted from 1962 edition. New York: New American Library, 1968.

Popper, K.R. *The Open Society and Its Enemies*, 2 vols. Reprinted from 1945 edition. Princeton: Princeton University Press, 1971.

Schoeck, Helmut. *Envy: A Theory of Social Behavior.* Translated from 1966 edition. New York: Harcourt Brace, 1970.

Rand, Ayn. *Anthem.* Reprinted from 1938 editon. New York: New American Library, 1974.

—*Atlas Shrugged.* Reprintd from 1957 edition. New York: New American Library, 1970.

—*Capitalism: The Unknown Ideal.* Reprinted from 1966 edition. New York: Signet Books, 1967.

—*The Virtue of Selfishness.* Reprinted from 1961 edition. New York: New American Library, 1973.

Reagan, Ronald. *Where's the Rest of Me?.* Reprinted from 1965 edition. New York: Dell Publishing Co., 1981.

Regnery, Henry. *Memoirs of a Dissident Publisher.* New York: Harcourt, Brace and Jovanovich, 1979.

Röpke, Wilhelm. *A Humane Economy: The Social Framework of the Free Market.* Chicago: Regnery Gateway, 1960.

—*The Social Crisis of Our Times.* Chicago: University of Chicago Press, 1950.

Rossiter, Clinton. *Conservatism in America: The Thankless Persuasion.* New York: Alfred A. Knopf, Inc., 1955.

Rothbard, Murray. *For a New Liberty: The Libertarian Manifesto.* New York: Macmillan Collier Books, 1973.

—*Man, Economy and State: A Treatise on Economic Principles.* Los Angeles: Nash Publishing Corp., 1961.

Rusher, William A. *The Making of the New Majority Party.* Ottawa, Ill.: Green Hill Publishers, 1975.

—*The Rise of the Right.* New York: William Morrow & Co., 1984.

Santayana, George. *Dominions and Powers.* New York: Charles Scribner's Sons, 1950.

Simons, Henry. *Economic Policy for a Free Society.* Chicago: University of Chicago Press, 1948.

Solzhenitsyn, Aleksandr. *The Gulag Archipelgo.* New York: Harper & Row Publishers, 1979.

—*One Day in the Life of Ivan Denisovich.* New York: Praeger Publishers, 1963.
Strauss, Leo. *Natural Right and History.* Chicago: University of Chicago Press, 1950.
—*The Political Philosophy of Hobbes: Its Basis and Its Genesis.* Chicago: University of Chicago Press, 1952.
—*Thoughts on Machiavelli.* Glencoe, Ill.: Free Press, 1958.
Toledano, Ralph de, and Victor Lasky. *Seeds of Treason: The Story of the Hiss-Chambers Case.* New York: Funk and Wagnalls Co., 1950.
Twelve Southerners. *I'll Take My Stand.* New York: Harper's, 1930.
Van den Haag, Ernest. *The Fabric of Society.* New York: Harcourt Brace, 1957.
—*Passion and Social Constraint.* New York: Stein and Day Publishers, 1963.
Viereck, Peter. *Conservatism: From John Adams to Churchill.* Princeton: D. Van Nostrand Co., 1956.
—*Conservatism Revisited.* Glencoe, Ill.: Free Press, 1962.
Voegelin, Eric. *The New Science of Politics: An Introduction.* Chicago: University of Chicago Press, 1952.
—*Order and History,* 4 vols. Baton Rouge: Louisiana State University Press, 1956–71.
Weaver, Richard M. *Ideas Have Consequences.* Chicago: University of Chicago Press, 1948.
Wilson, Francis Graham. *The Case for Conservatism.* Seattle: University of Washington Press, 1951.

SECOND GENERATION BOOKS

Allen, Richard V. and David M. Abshire, editors. *National Security: Political, Military and Economic Strategies in the Decade Ahead.* Stanford: Hoover Institution Press, 1963.
Anderson, Martin. *The Federal Bulldozer.* Cambridge, Mass.: MIT Press, 1964.
—*Welfare: The Political Economy of Welfare Reform in the United States.* Stanford: Hoover Institution Press, 1978.

Banfield, Edward. *The Unheavenly City.* Boston: Little, Brown & Co., 1968.

Barron, John. *KGB: The Secret Work of Soviet Secret Agents.* New York: Bantam Books, 1974.

Bartlett, Bruce. *Reaganomics: Supply-Side Economics in Action.* Westport, Conn.: Arlington House Publishers, 1981.

Bartlett, Bruce and Timothy Roth, editors. *The Supply-Side Solution.* Chatham, N.J.: Chatham House Publishers, 1983.

Bradford, M. E. *A Better Guide than Reason: Studies in the American Revolution.* La Salle, Ill.: Sherwood Sugden & Co., 1979.

—*A Worthy Company.* Marlborough, N.H.: Plymouth Rock Foundation, 1982.

—*The Generations of the Faithful Heart: On the Literature of the South.* La Salle, Ill.: Sherwood Sugden & Co., 1983.

—*Remembering Who We Are.* Athens: University of Georgia Press, 1985.

Buchanan, Patrick. *Conservative Voters, Liberal Victories: Why the Right Has Failed.* New York: Quadrangle/New York Times Book Co., 1975.

Butler, Stuart. *Enterprise Zones: Greenlining the Inner Cities.* New York: Universe Books, 1981.

—*Privatizing Federal Spending.* New York: Universe Books, 1985.

Conquest, Robert. *Present Danger: Towards a Foreign Policy.* Stanford: Hoover Institution Press, 1979.

—*The Great Terror: Stalin's Purge of the Thirties.* New York: Macmillan Publishing Co., 1968.

Cord, Robert. *Separation of Church and State: Historical Fact and Current Fiction.* New York: Lambeth Press, 1982.

Decter, Midge. *Liberal Parents, Radical Children.* New York: Coward, McCann and Geohegan, Inc., 1971.

—*Liberated Women and Other Americans.* New York: Coward, McCann and Geohegan, 1971.

Epstein, Richard. *Takings: Private Property and the Power of Eminent Domain.* Cambridge: Harvard University Press, 1985.

Evans, M. Stanton. *The Future of Conservatism.* New York: Holt, Rinehart and Winston, 1968.

—*The Liberal Establishment.* New York: Devin-Adair Co., 1965.
Feulner, Edwin J., Jr. *Conservatives Stalk the House.* Ottawa, Ill.: Green Hill Publishers, 1983.
Gilder, George. *Men and Marriage.* Revised from 1973 edition, entitled *Sexual Suicide.* Gretna, La.: Pelican Publishing Co., 1986.
—*Wealth and Poverty.* New York: Basic Books, 1982.
Hart, Jeffrey. *The American Dissent: A Decade of Modern Conservatism.* Garden City, N.Y.: Doubleday, 1966.
—*When the Going Was Good: American Life in the Fifties.* New York: Crown Publishers, 1981.
—*From This Moment On.* New York: Crown Publishers, 1987.
Himmelfarb, Gertrude. *Lord Acton: A Study in Conscience and Politics.* Chicago: University of Chicago Press, 1952.
—*On Liberty and Liberalism: The Case of John Stuart Mill.* New York: Alfred A. Knopf, Inc., 1974.
Hollander, Paul. *Political Pilgrims: Travels of Western Intellectuals to the Soviet Union, China and Cuba, 1928–1978.* Chicago: New University Press, 1981.
Jaffa, Harry V. *American Conservatism and the American Founding.* Durham: Carolina Academic Press, 1984.
—*Crisis of the House Divided: An Interpretation of the Issues in the Lincoln-Douglas Debates.* Garden City, N.Y.: Doubleday, 1959.
—*How to Think About the American Revolution: A Bicentennial Celebration.* Durham: Carolina Academic Press, 1978.
Johnson, Paul. *Modern Times: The World from the Twenties to the Eighties.* New York: Harper & Row Publishers, 1983.
Kemp, Jack. *The American Renaissance.* New York: Harper & Row Publishers, 1979.
Kirkpatrick, Jeane. *Dictatorships and Double Standards.* New York: American Enterprise Institute and Simon & Schuster, 1982.
Kristol, Irving. *On the Democratic Idea in America.* New York: Harper & Row Publishers, 1972.
—*Reflections of a Neoconservative: Looking Back, Looking Ahead.* New York: Basic Books, 1983.
—*Two Cheers for Capitalism.* New York: Signet Books, 1979.

LaHaye, Tim. *The Battle for the Mind.* Old Tappan, N.J.: Fleming H. Revell, 1980.

Lora, Ronald. *Conservatism in America.* Chicago: University of Chicago Press, 1971.

McDonald, Forrest. *Alexander Hamilton: A Biography.* New York: W.W. Norton & Co., 1982.

—*E Pluribus Unum.* Indianapolis: Liberty Press, 1979.

—*Novus Ordo Seclorum: The Intellectual Origins of the Constitution.* Lawrence: University Press of Kansas, 1985.

—*We the People.* Chicago: University of Chicago Press, 1976.

Murray, Charles. *Losing Ground: American Social Policy, 1950–1980.* New York: Basic Books, 1984.

Nash, George H. *The Conservative Intellectual Movement in America Since 1945.* New York: Basic Books, 1976.

Neuhaus, Richard J. *Christian Faith and Public Policy: Thinking and Acting in the Courage of Uncertainty.* Minneapolis: Augsburg Publishing House, 1977.

—*The Naked Public Square: Religion and Democracy in America.* Grand Rapids: Wilson B. Eerdmans Publishing Co, 1984.

Novak, Michael. *Freedom with Justice: Social Thought and Liberal Institutions.* New York: Harper & Row Publishers, 1984.

—*Moral Clarity in the Nuclear Age.* Nashville: Thomas Nelson, Inc., 1983.

—*The Spirit of Democratic Capitalism.* New York: Simon and Schuster, 1982.

Nozick, Robert. *Anarchy, State and Utopia.* New York: Basic Books, 1974.

Pines, Burton Yale. *Back to Basics.* New York: William Morrow & Co., 1982.

Pirie, Madsen. *The Book of the Fallacy: A Training Manual for Subversives.* Boston: Routledge and Kegan, 1983.

—*Dismantling the State.* Dallas: National Center for Policy Analysis, 1985.

—*Trial and Error and the Idea of Progress.* La Salle, Ill.: Open Court, 1978.

Podhoretz, Norman. *At the Bloody Crossroads.* New York: Simon and Schuster, 1986.

—*Breaking Ranks: A Political Memoir.* New York: Harper & Row Publishers, 1980.
—*The Present Danger.* New York: Simon and Schuster, 1980.
Revel, Jean-Francois. *How Democracies Perish.* Garden City, N.Y.: Doubleday, 1984.
—*The Totalitarian Temptation.* Garden City, N.Y.: Doubleday, 1977.
Rood, Harold. *Kingdoms of the Blind.* Durham: Carolina Academic Press, 1980.
Rueda, Enrique T. *The Homosexual Network.* Greenwich, Conn.: Devin-Adair Co., 1982.
Rushdoony, Rousas John. *Christianity and the State.* Vallecito, Ca.: Ross House Books, 1986.
—*Law and Liberty.* Vallecito, Ca.: Ross House Books, 1984.
Schaefer, Francis. *How Should We Then Live?: The Rise and Decline of Western Thought and Culture.* Old Tappan, N.J.: Fleming H. Revell Co., 1976.
Schlafly, Phyllis. *A Choice, Not an Echo.* Alton, Ill.: Pere Marquette Press, 1964.
Schuettinger, Robert. *Lord Acton: Historian of Liberty.* La Salle, Ill.: Open Court Publishing Co., 1976.
Siegan, Bernard H. *Economic Liberties and the Constitution.* Chicago: University of Chicago Press, 1980.
Simon, Julian L. and Herman Kahn, editors. *The Resourceful Earth.* New York: Basil Blackwell, 1984.
Simon, William. *A Time for Truth.* New York: McGraw Hill Book Co., 1978.
Sowell, Thomas. *Ethnic America.* New York: Basic Books, 1981.
—*Markets and Minorities.* New York: Basic Books, 1981.
—*Marxism: Philosophy and Economics.* New York: William Morrow & Co., 1985.
—*Race and Economics.* New York: McKay, David Co., 1975.
Tyrrell, R. Emmett. (ed.) *The Future that Doesn't Work.* Garden City, NY Doubleday, 1975.
—*The Liberal Crack-Up.* New York: Simon and Schuster, 1984.
—*Public Nuisances.* New York: Basic Books, 1979.

Tyson, James L. *Target America: The Influence of Communist Propaganda on U.S. Media.* Chicago: Regnery Gateway, 1982.
Viguerie, Richard. *The Establishment Versus the People: Is a New Populist Revolt on the Way?.* Chicago: Regnery Gateway, 1983.
—*The New Right: We're Ready to Lead.* Falls Church, Va.: Caroline House, 1980.
Wanniski, Jude. *The Way the World Works: How Economies Fail and Succeed.* New York: Basic Books, 1978.
Weinstein, Allen. *Perjury: The Hiss-Chambers Case.* New York: Alfred A. Knopf, Inc., 1978.
Will, George F. *The Pursuit of Happiness and Other Sobering Thoughts.* New York: Harper & Row Publishers, 1979.
—*The Pursuit of Virtue and Other Tory Notions.* New York: Simon and Schuster, 1982.
Williams, Walter. *America: A Minority Viewpoint.* Stanford: Hoover Institution Press, 1982.
—*The State Against Blacks.* New York: McGraw Hill Book Co., 1982.
Wilson, Clyde, editor. *Why the South Will Survive.* Athens: University of Georgia Press, 1981.
Wilson, James Q. *Thinking About Crime.* New York: Basic Books, 1975.
Wolfe, Tom. *Radical Chic and Mau-Mauing the Flak Catchers.* New York: Farrar, Straus & Giroux, 1970.

THIRD GENERATION BOOKS

Bandow, Doug, editor. *Protecting the Environment: A Free Market Strategy.* Washington, D.C.: The Heritage Foundation, 1986.
—editor. *U.S. Aid to the Developing World.* Washington, D.C.: The Heritage Foundation, 1985.
Brookhiser, Richard. *The Outside Story: How Democrats and Republicans Reelected Reagan.* Garden City, N.Y.: Doubleday, 1986.
D'Souza, Dinesh. *Before the Millennium: A Critical Biography of Jerry Falwell.* Chicago: Regnery Gateway, 1984.

—*Catholic Classics*. Huntington, Ind.: Our Sunday Visitor Press, 1986.
Ferrara, Peter. *Religion and the Constitution: A Reinterpretation*. Washington, D.C.: Child and Family Protection Institute, 1983.
—*Social Security: Averting the Crisis*. Washington, D.C.: Cato Institute, 1981.
—*Social Security: The Inherent Contradiction*. Washington, D.C.: Cato Institute, 1982.
—editor. *Social Security: Prospects for Reform*. Washington, D.C.: Cato Institute, 1981.
Fossedal, Gregory, and Lt. Gen. Daniel O. Graham. *A Defense that Defends*. Greenwich, Conn.: Devin-Adair Co., 1984.
Hart, Benjamin. *Poisoned Ivy*. New York: Stein and Day Publishers, 1984.
McGuigan, Patrick. *A Blueprint for Judicial Reform*. Washington, D.C.: Free Congress Research and Education Foundation, 1981.
—*Criminal Justice Reform: A Blueprint*. Washington, D.C.: Free Congress Research and Education Foundation, 1983.
—*The Politics of Direct Democracy in the 1980s: Case Studies in Popular Decision Making*. Washington, D.C.: The Institute on Government and Politics, 1985.
Meyerson, Adam, and David Asman, editors. *The Wall Street Journal on Management*. New York: Dow Jones Books, 1985.
Vigilante, Richard, editor. *Consumer Issues of the Eighties*. Washington, D.C.: Consumers Research, 1980.
Vigilante, Richard, and Gregory Sandford. *Grenada: The Untold Story*. Lanham, Md.: Scribners Madison Publishers, 1984.
Waller, J. Michael. *The Revolution Lobby*. Washington, D.C.: Council for Inter-American Security, 1985.

CLASSICS

Acton, Lord. *Essays on Freedom and Power*. London: Meridian, 1956. Lord Acton died in 1902 without ever having published a book. His essays and notes on history and politics were collected posthumously and published in various forms.

Adams, John. *The Political Writings of John Adams,* which contains his *Defense of the American Constitution.* Edited by George A. Peek, Jr. Indianapolis: Bobbs, Merrill Co., 1954.

Aristotle. *Politics.* 330 B.C. (many editions).

Bastiat, Frederic. *Economic Sophisms.* 1843–1850 (many editions).

The Bible (many editions).

Boswell, James. *Life of Johnson.* 1791 (many editions).

Brownson, Orestes A. *The American Republic.* 1866. Edited by Americo D. Lapatis. New Haven: New Haven College University Press, 1972.

Burke, Edmund. *Reflections on the Revolution in France.* 1789 (many editions).

Calhoun, John C. *A Disquisition on Government.* 1845. Indianapolis: The Bobbs-Merrill Company, 1953. While his defense of slavery is antithetical to prinicples enunciated in the Declaration of Independence and has severely soiled his reputation in history, it would be a mistake to ignore his brilliant defense of states' rights as a check on the centralizing tendency of the federal government.

Cooper, James Fenimore. *The American Democrat.* 1838. Indianapolis: Liberty Classics, 1981.

The Constitution of the United States of America. 1787–88.

The Declaration of Independence. 1776.

Emerson, Ralph Waldo. *Essays on Wealth and Politics* (many editions).

The Federalist Papers. Alexander Hamilton, John Jay, and James Madison. 1787 (many editions).

Hobbes, Thomas. *Leviathan.* 1651 (many editions). While many conservatives are repelled by Hobbes's defense of the omnipotent, centralized state, they agree there is much truth in his assessment of man's corrupt nature and life being "nasty, brutish and short."

Hume, David. *Essays: Moral, Political and Literary.* 1777. Indianapolis: Liberty Classics, 1985.

Jefferson, Thomas. See *The Portable Thomas Jefferson.* Contains his

"Notes on the State of Virginia." Edited by Merrill D. Peterson. New York: Penguin Books.

Locke, John. *Two Treatises of Government.* 1690 (many editions).

Madison, James. *Reports of Debates in the Federal Convention.* 1787 (many editions).

Mallock, William Hurrell. *Is Life Worth Living?* London: Chatto and Windus, 1880.

—*The New Republic.* London: Michael Joseph, 1887.

Mill, John Stuart. *On Liberty.* 1859 (many editions).

Montesquieu, Baron de. *The Spirit of the Laws.* 1748 (many editions).

Paine, Thomas. *Common Sense.* 1776 (many editions).

Smith, Adam. *The Theory of Moral Sentiments.* 1759 (many editions).

—*The Wealth of Nations.* 1776 (many editions).

Spencer, Herbert. *The Man vs. the State.* 1884 (many editions).

Stephen, James Fitzjames. *Liberty, Equality, Fraternity.* London: Smith, Elder and Co., 1873.

Tocqueville, Alexis de. *Democracy in America.* 1835 (many editions).